Best Editorial Cartoons of the Year

CURATOLO EDMONTON SUN

FRED CURATOLO
Courtesy Edmonton Sun

BEST EDITORIAL CARTOONS OF THE YEAR

1998 EDITION

Edited by
CHARLES BROOKS

PELICAN PUBLISHING COMPANY
Gretna 1998

Library of Congress Serial Catalog Data

Best editorial cartoons. 1972-
    Gretna La. Pelican Pub. Co.
    v. 29 cm annual-
"A pictorial history of the year."

    1. United States—Politics and government—
1969—Caricatures and Cartoons—Periodicals.
E839.5.B45   320.9'7309240207   73-643645
ISNN 0091-2220   MARC-s

Manufactured in the United States of America
Published by Pelican Publishing Company, Inc.
P.O. Box 3110, Gretna, Louisiana 70054-3110

Contents

Award-Winning Cartoons

1997 PULITZER PRIZE

WALT HANDELSMAN

Editorial Cartoonist
New Orleans Times-Picayune

Born 1956; graduated from the University of Cincinnati; cartoonist for 13 suburban weekly newspapers in the Washington-Baltimore area, 1982-85, the Scranton *Times*, 1985-89, and the New Orleans *Times-Picayune*, 1989 to the present; cartoons appear in more than 100 newspapers; winner of the National Headliner Award, 1989 and 1993, the Society of Professional Journalists/Sigma Delta Chi Award, 1992, and the Robert F. Kennedy Journalism Award, 1996; author of a children's book and two collections of editorial cartoons.

1997 FISCHETTI AWARD

GARY MARKSTEIN

Editorial Cartoonist
Milwaukee Journal Sentinel

Born January 6, 1959, in Ridgewood, New Jersey; graduated from
Arizona State University, 1982; editorial cartoonist for the Tribune
Newspapers of Arizona, 1986-91, and the Milwaukee *Journal Sentinel*,
1992 to the present; nationally syndicated by Copley News Service; win-
ner of the Milwaukee Press Club Award, 1992, 1994, and 1996, and the
Cox Newspapers Best Editorial Cartoonist Award, 1988.

1996 NATIONAL SOCIETY
OF PROFESSIONAL JOURNALISTS AWARD
(Awarded in 1997)

PAUL CONRAD

Editorial Cartoonist
Los Angeles Times Syndicate

Born in Cedar Rapids, Iowa, in 1924; graduated from the University of Iowa, 1950; editorial cartoonist for the Denver *Post*, 1950-64, the Los Angeles *Times*, 1964-93, and the Los Angeles *Times Syndicate*, 1964 to present; previous winner of the National Society of Professional Journalists/Sigma Delta Chi Award, 1963, 1969, 1971, 1981, 1982, and 1988, the Overseas Press Club Award, 1970 and 1981, the Pulitzer Prize, 1964, 1971, and 1984, and the Robert F. Kennedy Award, 1985, 1990, 1992, and 1993; author of five books; widely exhibited sculptor; his work is included in "American Treasures of the Library of Congress."

1997 NATIONAL HEADLINER AWARD

ANN TELNAES

Editorial Cartoonist
North American Syndicate

Born in Stockholm, Sweden, in 1960; graduated from the California Institute of the Arts; cartoons distributed by the North American Syndicate to more than 425 publications; winner of the Population Institute XVIIth Global Media Award, 1996, and the sixth annual Environmental Media Award for editorial cartooning.

1997 MENCKEN AWARD

RAMIREZ
LOS ANGELES TIMES
Presidential Quotations
I CANNOT TELL A LIE...
I CANNOT RECALL...
FOUR SCORE AND SEVEN YEARS AGO...
FIFTY THOUSAND AND THE LINCOLN BEDROOM IS YOURS...
ASK NOT WHAT YOUR COUNTRY CAN DO FOR YOU; ASK WHAT YOU CAN DO FOR YOUR COUNTRY...
ASK NOT WHAT OTHER COUNTRIES HAVE DONE FOR THE DEMOCRAT PARTY...
I AM NOT A CROOK.
I AM NOT A CROOK..

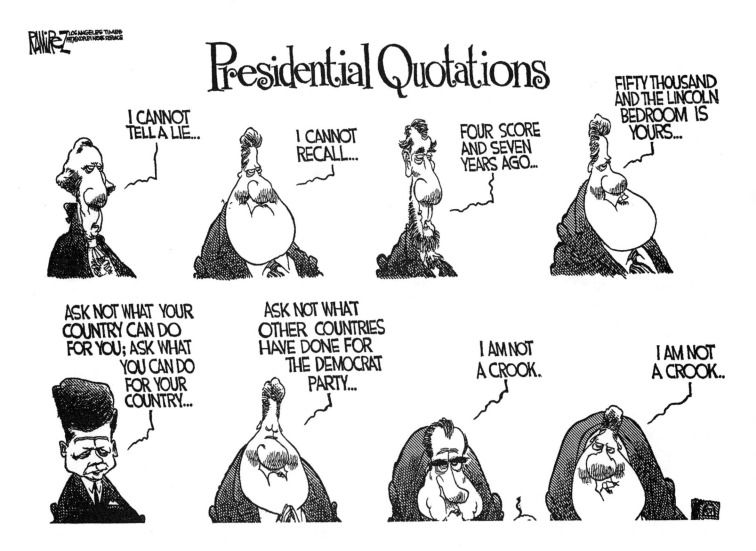

MICHAEL RAMIREZ

Editorial Cartoonist
Los Angeles Times

Born in Tokyo, Japan; graduated from the University of California at Irvine; editorial cartoonist for the Newport Ensign, the San Clemente *Daily Sun* and *Post*, and the Memphis *Commercial Appeal*, 1990-97; cartoonist for the Los Angeles *Times*, 1997 to the present; syndicated by Copley News Service; winner of the Pulitzer Prize, 1994, the Mencken Award, 1995, and the National Society of Professional Journalists Award, 1995.

1996 NATIONAL NEWSPAPER AWARD / CANADA
(Awarded in 1997)

ROY PETERSON

Editorial Cartoonist
Vancouver Sun

Born in Winnipeg, Manitoba, in 1936; editorial cartoonist for the
Vancouver *Sun*, 1962 to the present; previous five-time winner of the
National Newspaper Award of Canada; winner of the International Salon
of Cartoons Grand Prize, 1973; syndicated by Torstar of Canada and
Cartoonists and Writers of New York; and former president of the
Association of Canadian Editorial Cartoonists and the Association of
American Editorial Cartoonists.

Best Editorial Cartoons of the Year

PAUL CONRAD
Courtesy Los Angeles Times Syndicate

The Clinton Administration

Scandal continued to plague the Clinton White House, with startling revelations that the administration had granted access to the president in exchange for campaign donations. It was alleged that hefty contributions from the Chinese government were channeled through agents with ties to Indonesia. Clinton also met with potential contributors at high-priced "coffee klatches," and donors were rewarded with overnight stays in the Lincoln bedroom of the White House.

Attorney General Janet Reno was urged to appoint an independent counsel to investigate fund-raising activities, including telephone calls from the White House by Clinton and Vice-president Albert Gore. Evidence that the law had been broken repeatedly seemed overwhelming, but Reno announced that she found no such evidence.

The U.S. Supreme Court ruled that Paula Jones's sexual harassment suit against Clinton could proceed while the president was still in office. Clinton boasted that the 1999 budget would be balanced by cuts in spending and a growing economy, but two-thirds of the proposed cuts would not take effect until the year 2000.

Vice-president Gore issued an apology and admitted to a "miscommunication' when he told reporters that he and his wife, Tipper, were the models for Oliver and Jenny in the romance novel *Love Story*. Author Erich Segal insisted it was not so.

The Clinton war on drugs never got off the ground in 1997.

MICHAEL RAMIREZ
Courtesy Los Angeles Times

DICK WRIGHT
Courtesy Columbus Dispatch

JACK HIGGINS
Courtesy Chicago Sun-Times

MIKE SMITH
Courtesy United Features Syndicate

REX BABIN
Courtesy Albany Times Union

Berry's World

JIM BERRY
Courtesy NEA

MIKE LANE
Courtesy Baltimore Sun

ANN TELNAES
Courtesy Prince George's Journal

ANN TELNAES
ATelnaes@AOL.COM

MICHAEL RAMIREZ
Courtesy Los Angeles Times

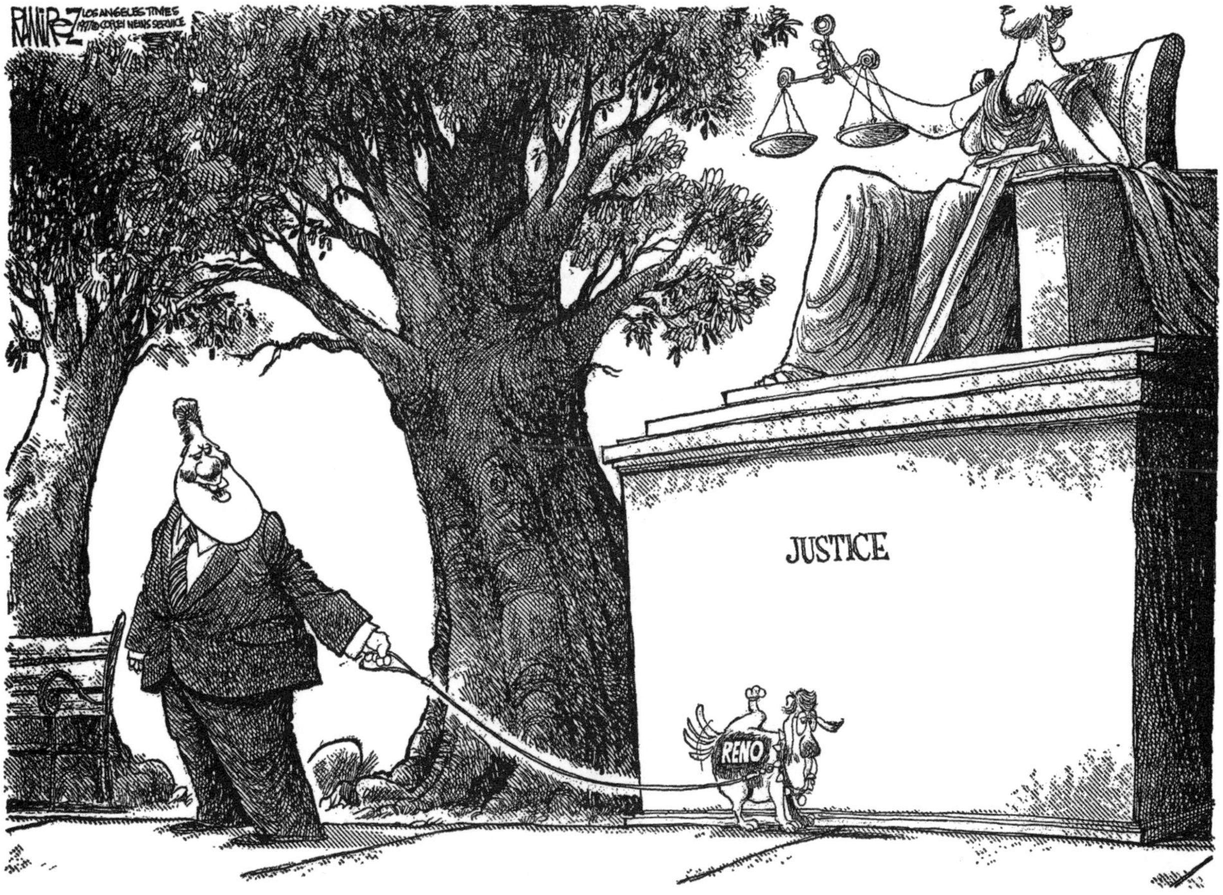
JUSTICE
RENO

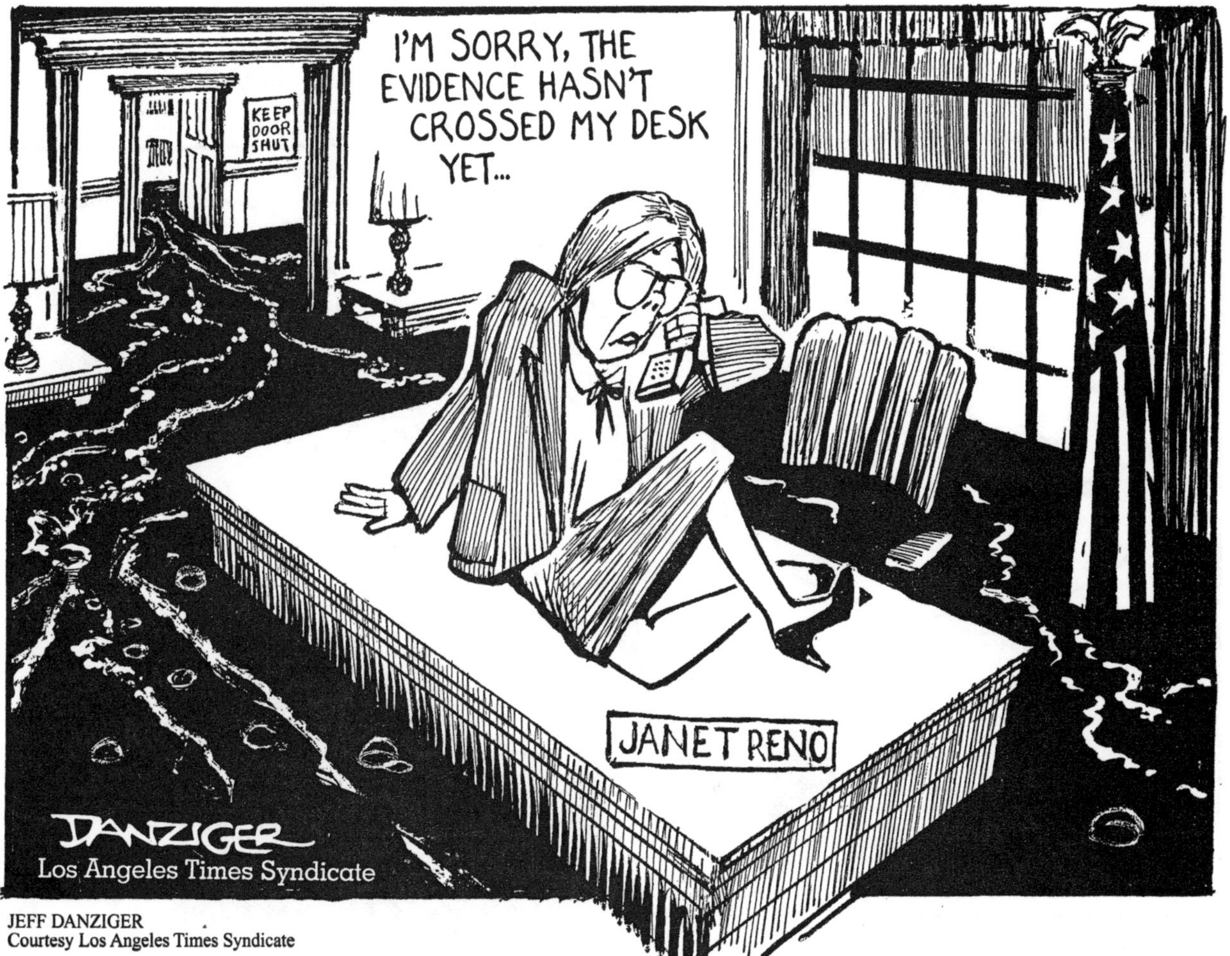
I'M SORRY, THE EVIDENCE HASN'T CROSSED MY DESK YET...
KEEP DOOR SHUT
JANET RENO
DANZIGER
Los Angeles Times Syndicate

JEFF DANZIGER
Courtesy Los Angeles Times Syndicate

Berry's World

ACTUALLY, WE THOUGHT IT WAS A 'FRUIT-OUTREACH' PROGRAM. THERE WAS NO 'INTENT' TO EAT THE APPLE. ALSO, THERE SEEMED TO BE 'NO CONTROLLING AUTHORITY' ...

© 1997 by NEA, Inc.

JIM BERRY
Courtesy NEA

MR PRESIDENT, PAULA JONES JUST SAID —

I CAN'T HEAR YOU!

©1997 BRANDON, JR. FLORIDA TODAY

BRUMSIC BRANDON, JR.
Courtesy Florida Today

JEFF MACNELLY
Courtesy Chicago Tribune
and Tribune Media Services

JOHN TREVER
Courtesy Albuquerque Journal

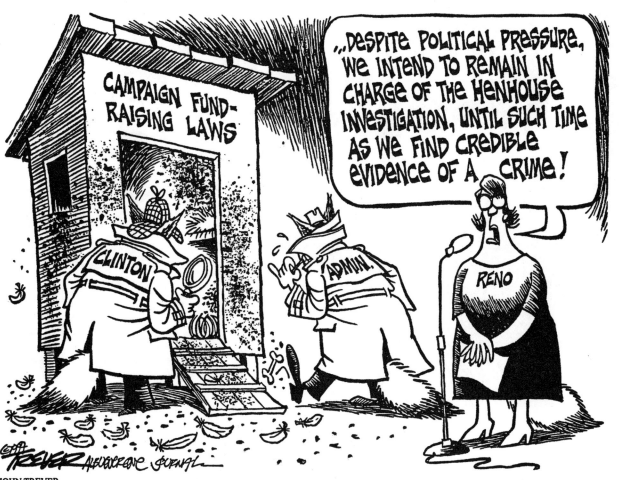

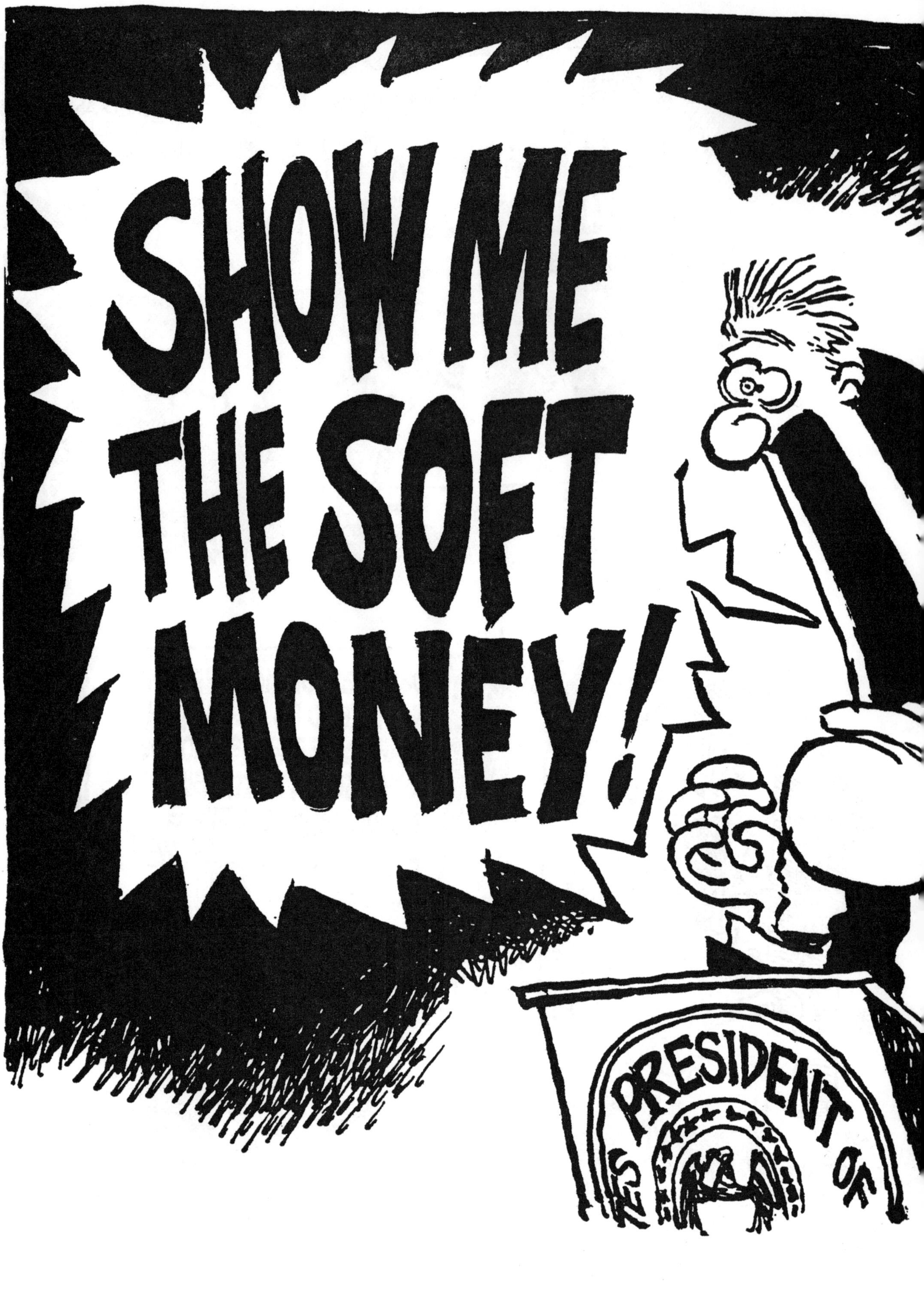
SHOW ME THE SOFT MONEY!
PRESIDENT OF

MIKE PETERS
Courtesy Dayton Daily News

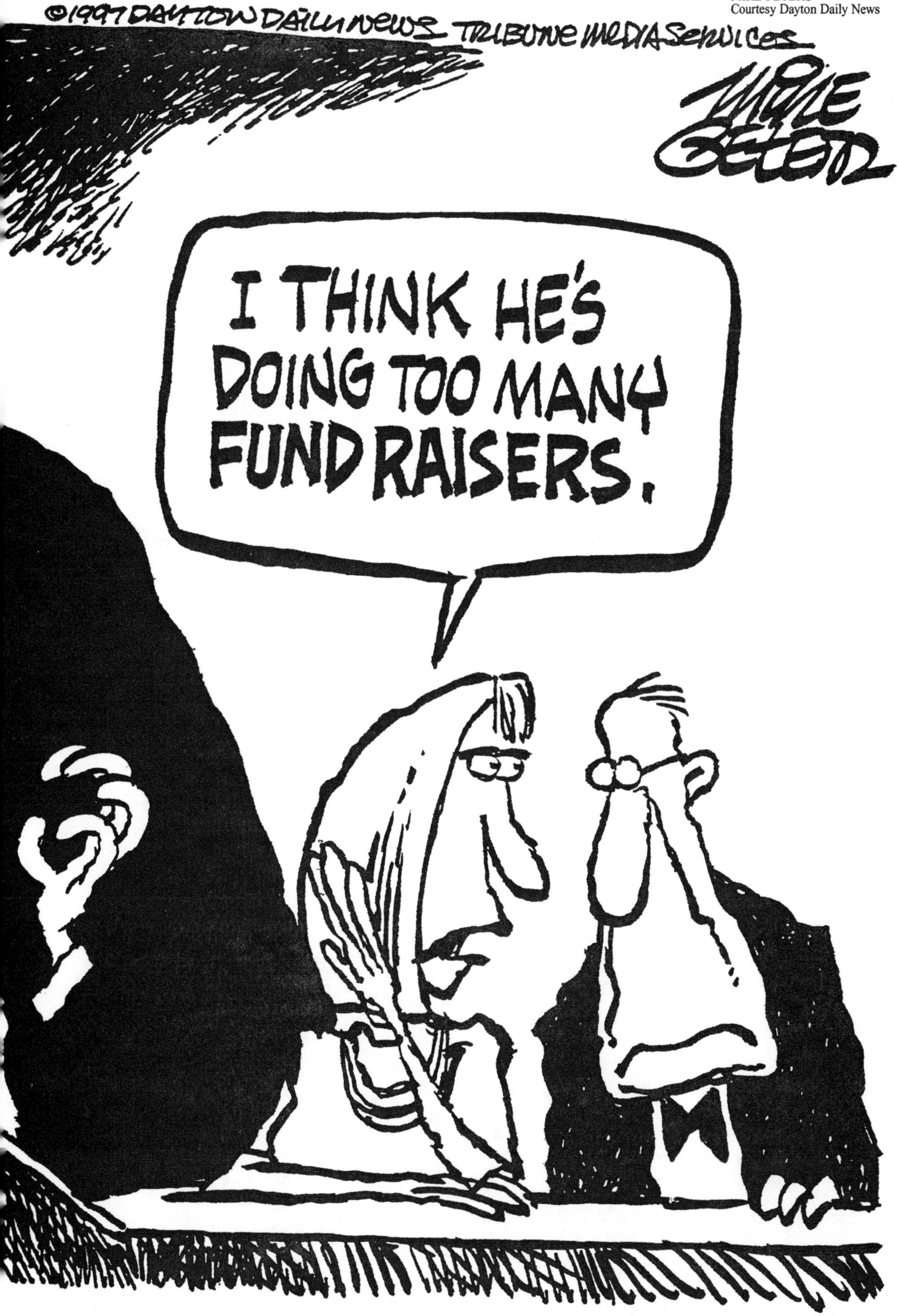
©1997 DAYTON DAILY NEWS TRIBUNE MEDIA SERVICES
MIKE PETERS
I THINK HE'S DOING TOO MANY FUND RAISERS.

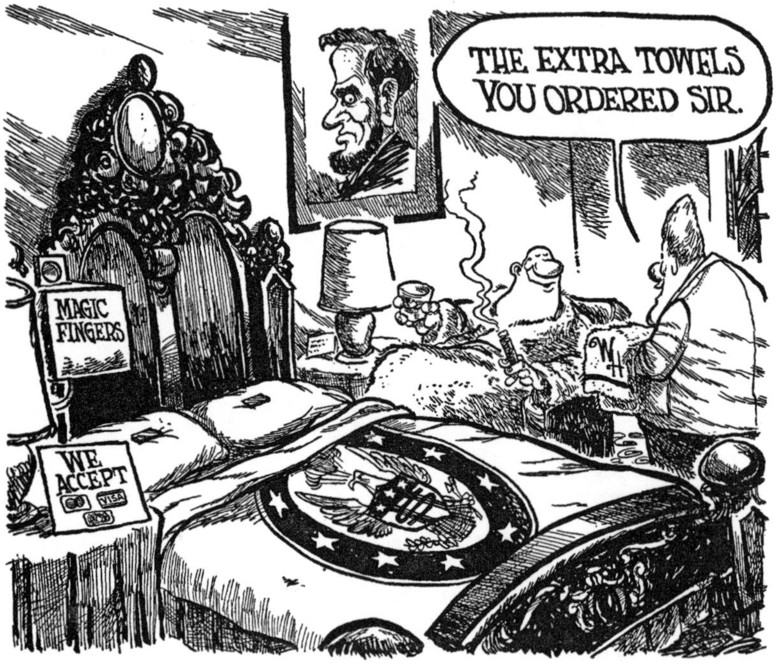
THE EXTRA TOWELS YOU ORDERED SIR.
MAGIC FINGERS
WE ACCEPT
VISA

BRIAN DUFFY
Courtesy Des Moines Register

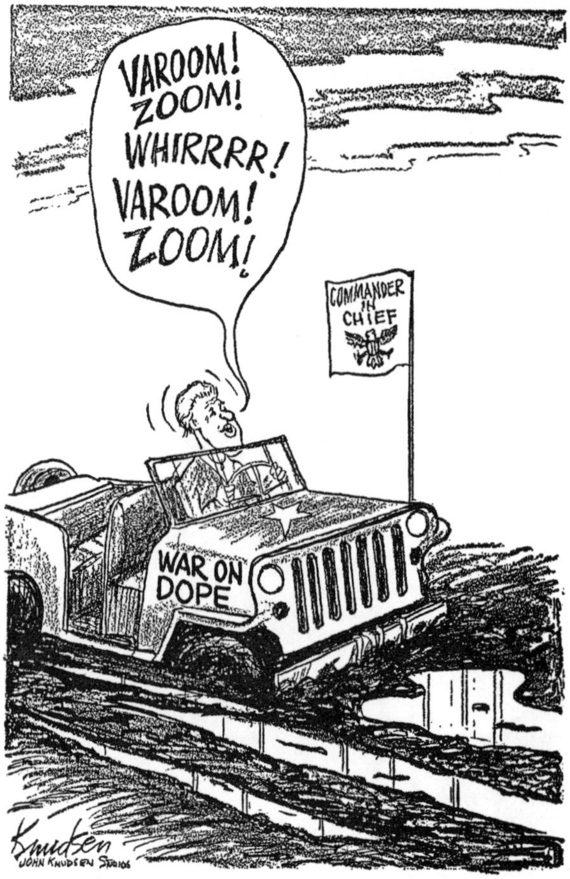
VAROOM! ZOOM! WHIRRRR! VAROOM! ZOOM!
COMMANDER IN CHIEF
WAR ON DOPE
Knudsen
JOHN KNUDSEN STUDIOS

JOHN J. KNUDSEN
Courtesy St. Louis Review

JIM BORGMAN
Courtesy Cincinnati Enquirer

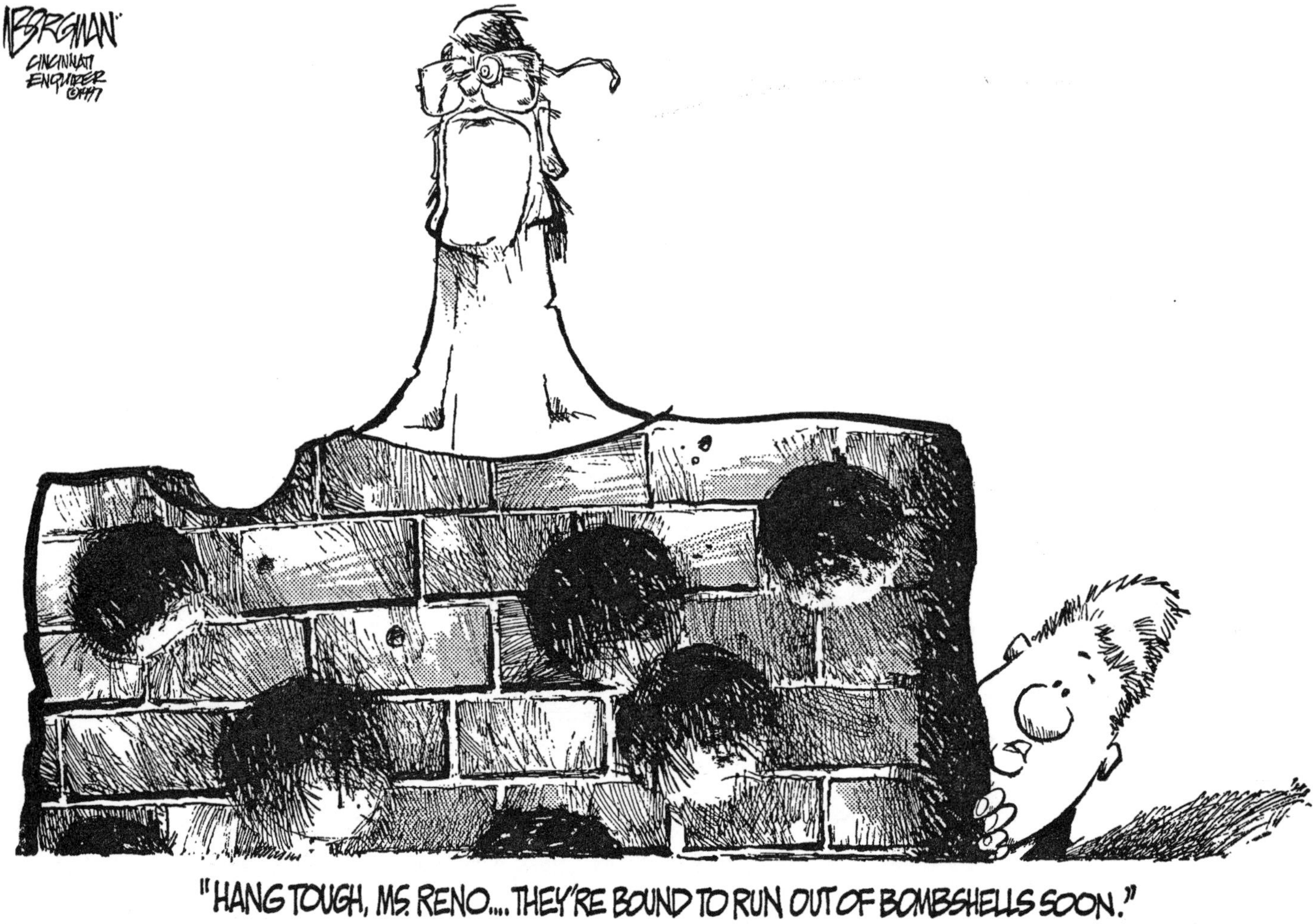
BORGMAN
CINCINNATI ENQUIRER ©1997

"HANG TOUGH, MS. RENO.... THEY'RE BOUND TO RUN OUT OF BOMBSHELLS SOON."

CHIP BOK
Courtesy Akron Beacon Journal

PETER DUNLAP-SHOHL
Courtesy Anchorage Daily News

DAVID GRANLUND
Courtesy Middlesex News (Mass.)

25

STEVE KELLEY
Courtesy San Diego Union-Tribune

CHUCK ASAY
Courtesy Colorado Springs Gazette Telegraph

THE GREAT RECONCILER — PERT'NEAR...

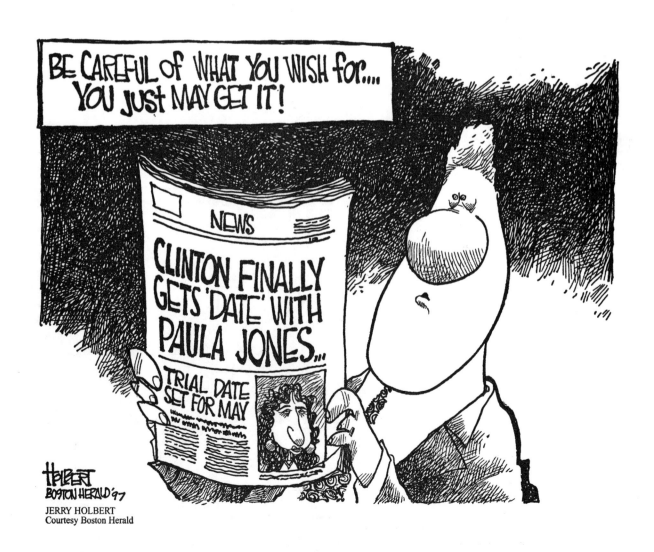

M. WUERKER
Courtesy Los Angeles Times

DICK LOCHER
Courtesy Chicago Tribune

DRAPER HILL
Courtesy Detroit News

28

SCOTT STANTIS
Courtesy Birmingham News

©1997 THE BIRMINGHAM NEWS
STANTIS

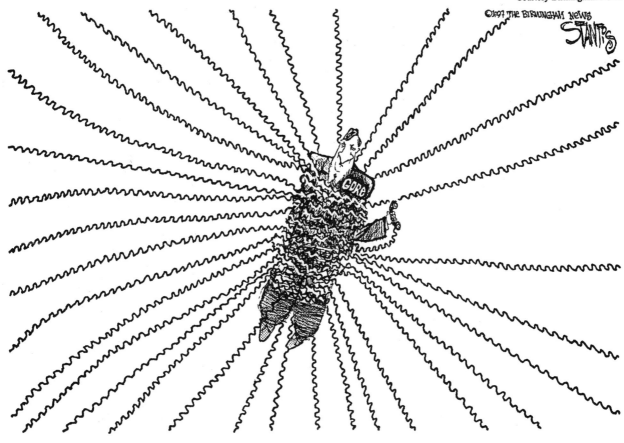

CLAY JONES
Courtesy Honolulu Star-Bulletin

29

MILT PRIGGEE
Courtesy Spokane Spokesman-Review

PAUL CONRAD
Courtesy Los Angeles Times Syndicate

BOB ENGLEHART
Courtesy Hartford Courant

JACK HIGGINS
Courtesy Chicago Sun-Times

CHARLIE DANIEL
Courtesy Knoxville News-Sentinel

"BILL, BILL, BILL OF THE JUNGLE"...

MILT PRIGGEE
Courtesy Spokane Spokesman-Review

IN TIMES OF TROUBLE, I'LL WANDER THROUGH THE ROSE GARDEN, STOP AND SMELL THE FLOWERS AND CONTEMPLATE MY **PRIORITIES.**

BOY, I BET CONTRIBUTORS WOULD PAY BIG FOR THIS...

JOHN KOVALIC
Courtesy State Journal (Wisc.)

MARSHALL RAMSEY
Courtesy Jackson Clarion-Ledger

LINCOLN BEDROOM

DEPOSIT CHECK HERE

"SORRY, SOCKS... ONLY FAT CATS ARE ALLOWED IN HERE."

JAKE FULLER
Courtesy Gainesville Sun

JEFF KOTERBA
Courtesy Omaha World-Herald

LARRY WRIGHT
Courtesy Detroit News

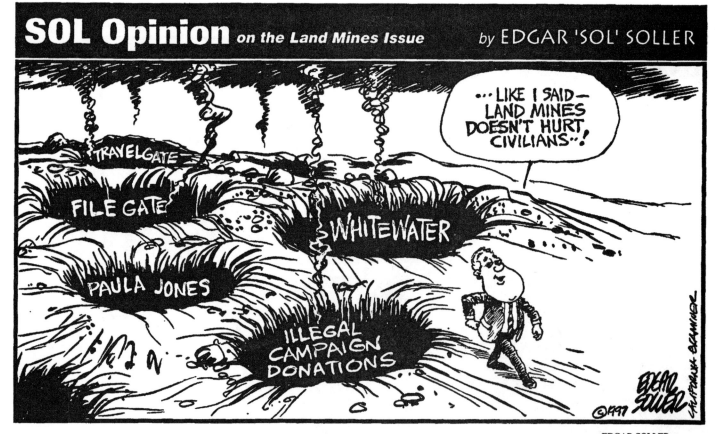

EDGAR SOLLER
Courtesy California Examiner

DICK LOCHER
Courtesy Chicago Tribune

JOE HELLER
Courtesy Green Bay Press-Gazette

**"Al, We'll Keep The Pressure On The Senate Republicans
To Do Something About 'Soft Money'"**

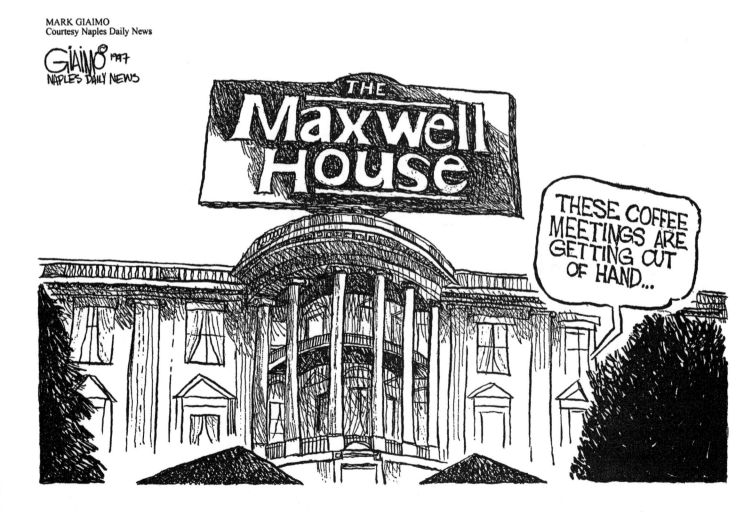

MIKE LUCKOVICH ATLANTA CONSTITUTION &97

AN AIDE MISPLACED HIS KEYS, SO HE CALLS FRIENDS TO HELP HIM GET IN. WELL, UNBEKNOWNST TO ME, THEY GO TO THE WRONG PLACE, JIMMY THE DOOR AND LO AND BEHOLD, IT'S THE WATERGATE!...

IF NIXON HANDLED SCANDALS LIKE CLINTON DOES

WILL WORK FOR FOOD

WILL WORK FOR COFFEE$

MARK THORNHILL
Courtesy North County Times (Calif.)

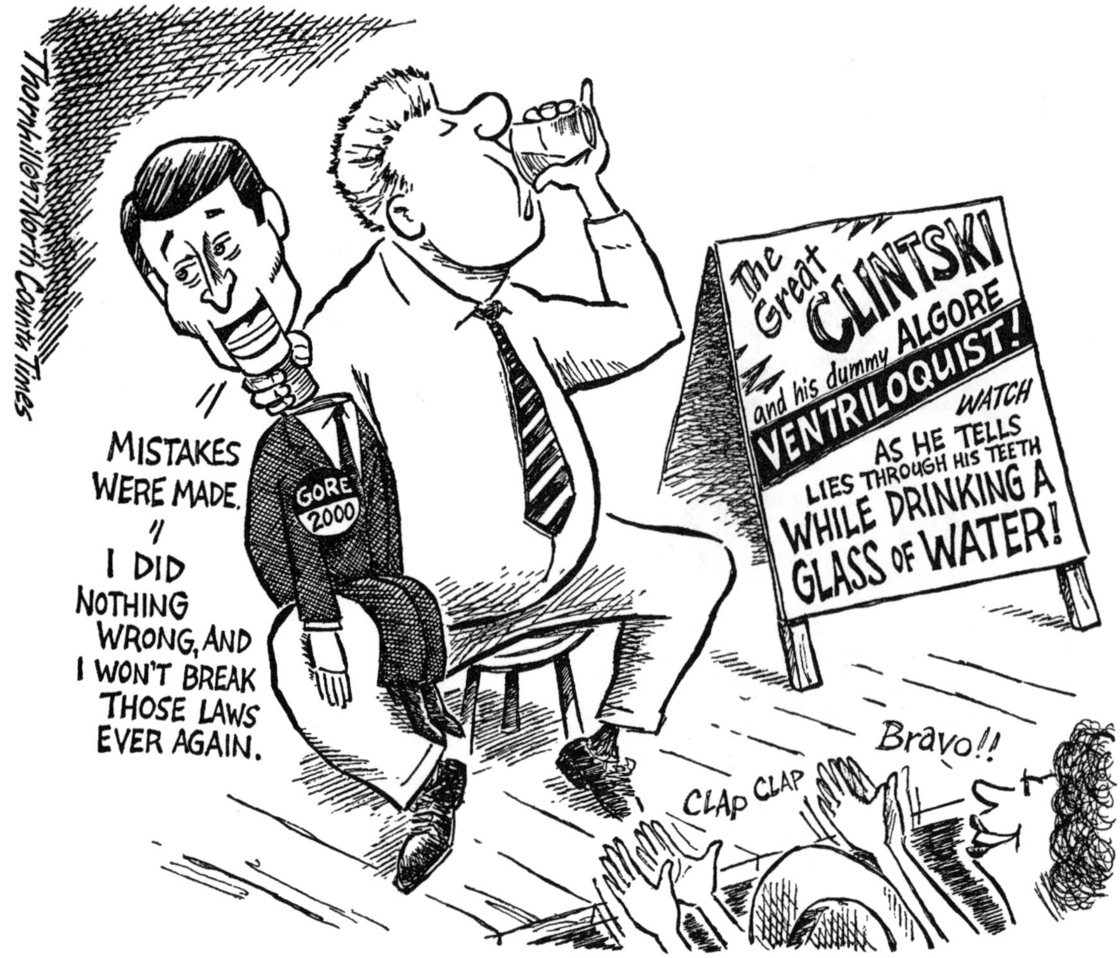

Thornhill©97North County Times
The Great CLINTSKI
and his dummy ALGORE
VENTRILOQUIST!
WATCH AS HE TELLS LIES THROUGH HIS TEETH WHILE DRINKING A GLASS OF WATER!
GORE 2000
"MISTAKES WERE MADE."
"I DID NOTHING WRONG, AND I WON'T BREAK THOSE LAWS EVER AGAIN."
Bravo!!
CLAP CLAP

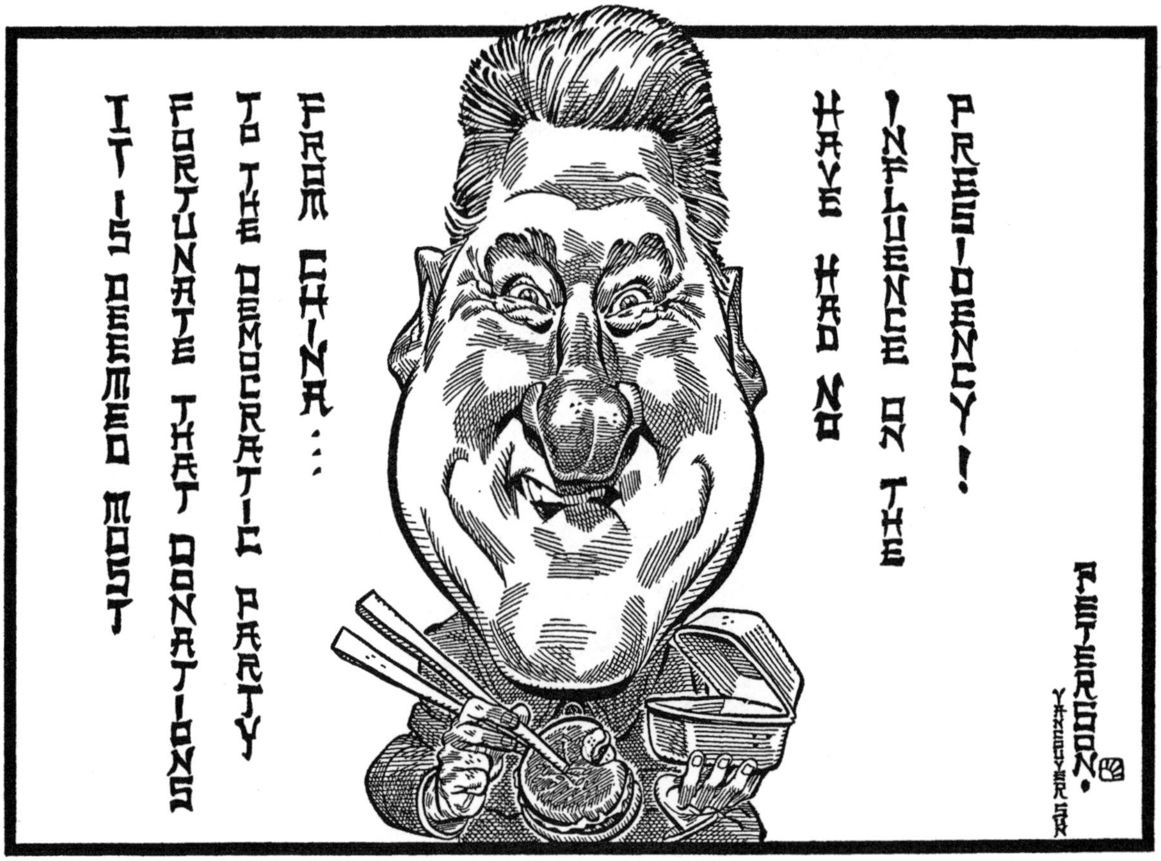

IT IS DEEMED MOST
FORTUNATE THAT DONATIONS
TO THE DEMOCRATIC PARTY
FROM CHINA...
HAVE HAD NO
INFLUENCE ON THE
PRESIDENCY!
PETERSON.
VANCOUVER SUN

ROY PETERSON
Courtesy Vancouver Sun

STEVE KELLEY
Courtesy San Diego Union-Tribune

JEFF NACNELLY
Courtesy Chicago Tribune
and Tribune Media Services

The Legacy Thing

Vice President Al Gore in China, filming future Gephardt-for-President spots.

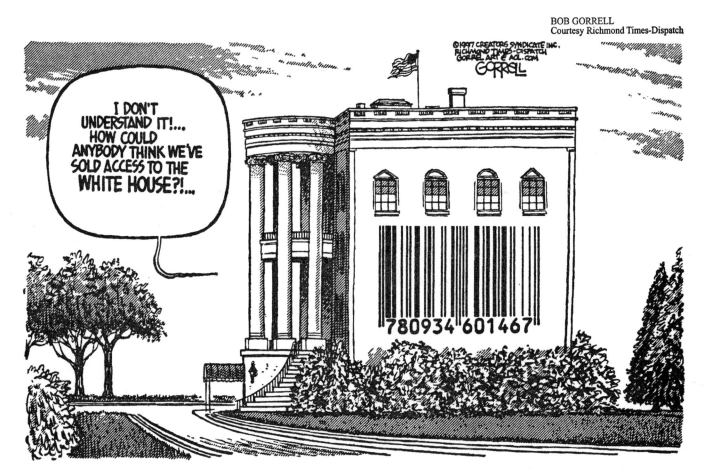

ROMON GENN
Courtesy National Review

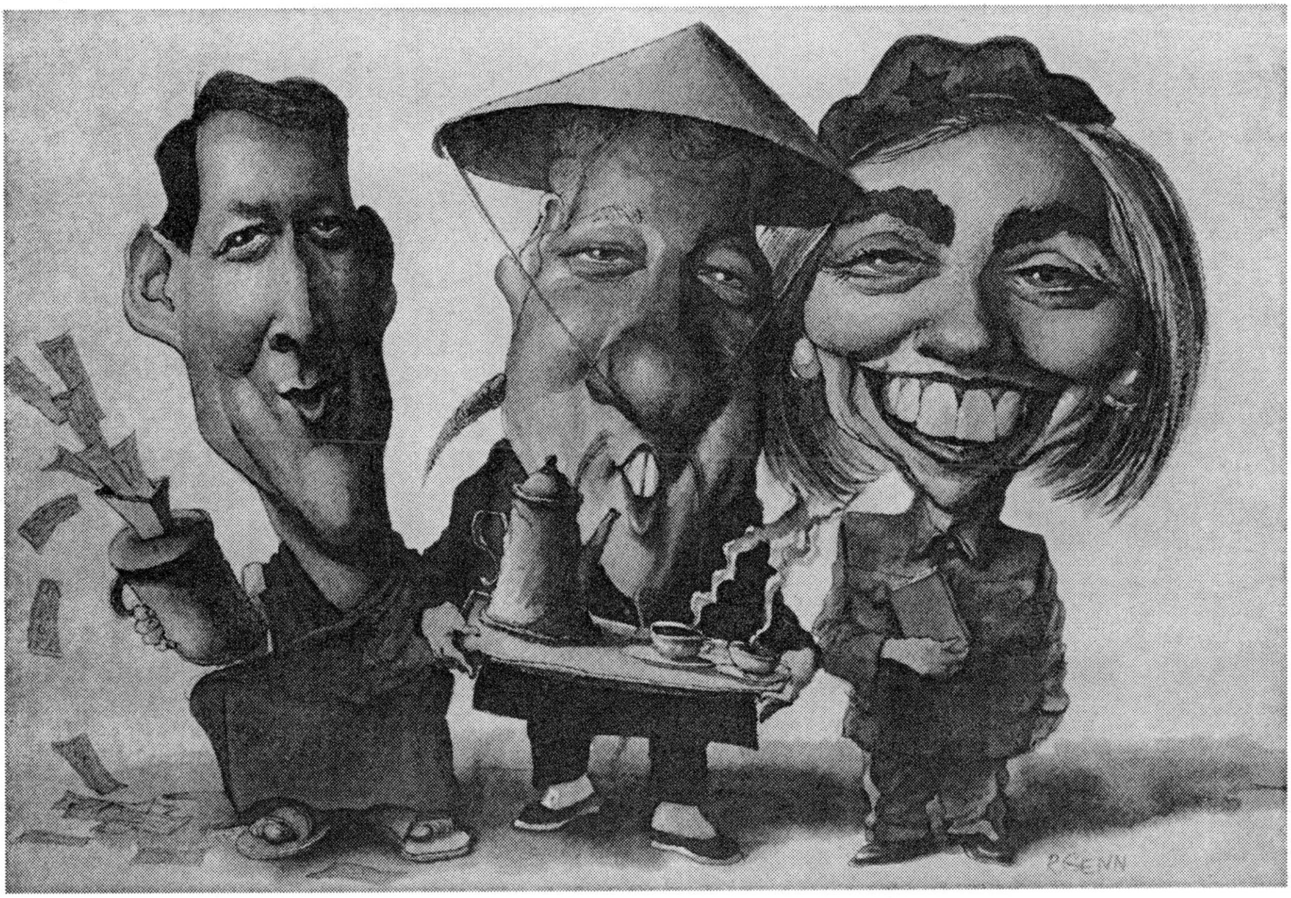
R GENN

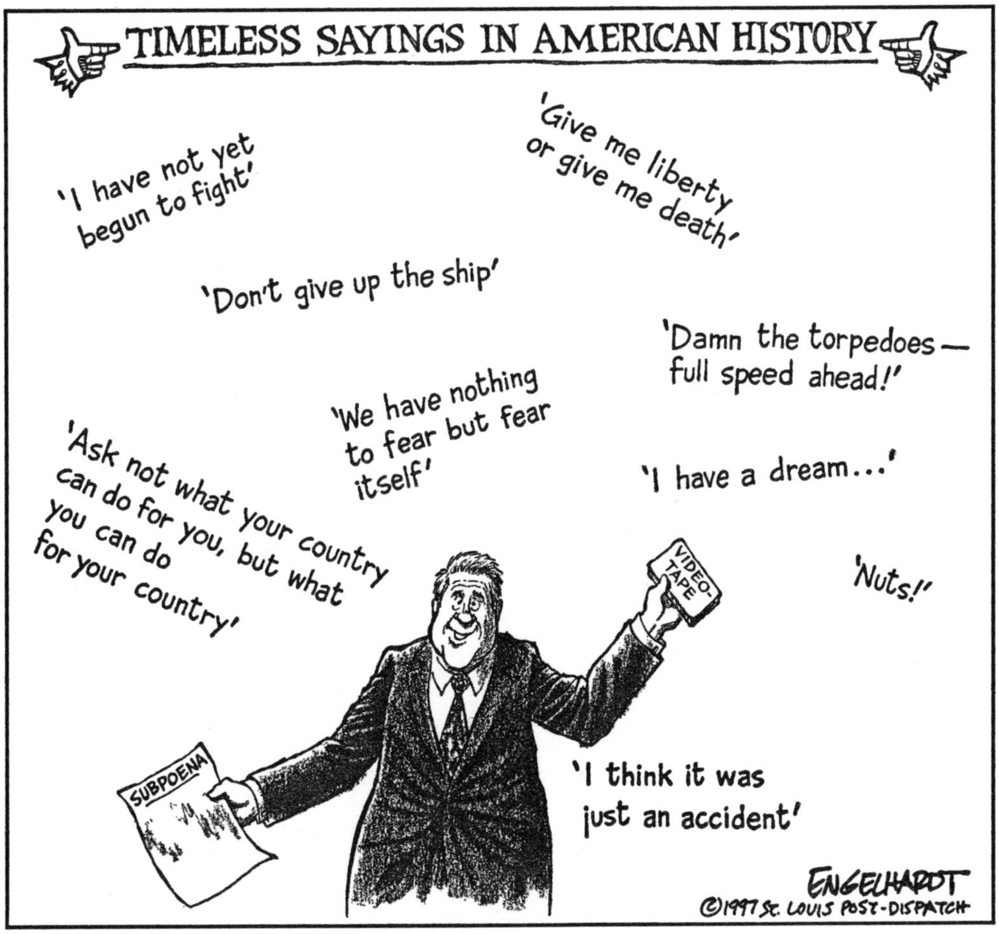
TIMELESS SAYINGS IN AMERICAN HISTORY
'I have not yet begun to fight'
'Give me liberty or give me death'
'Don't give up the ship'
'Damn the torpedoes— full speed ahead!'
'We have nothing to fear but fear itself'
'Ask not what your country can do for you, but what you can do for your country'
'I have a dream...'
'Nuts!'
VIDEO-TAPE
SUBPOENA
'I think it was just an accident'
ENGELHARDT
©1997 St. Louis Post-Dispatch

TOM ENGELHARDT
Courtesy St. Louis Post-Dispatch

JEFF MACNELLY
Courtesy Chicago Tribune
and Tribune Media Services

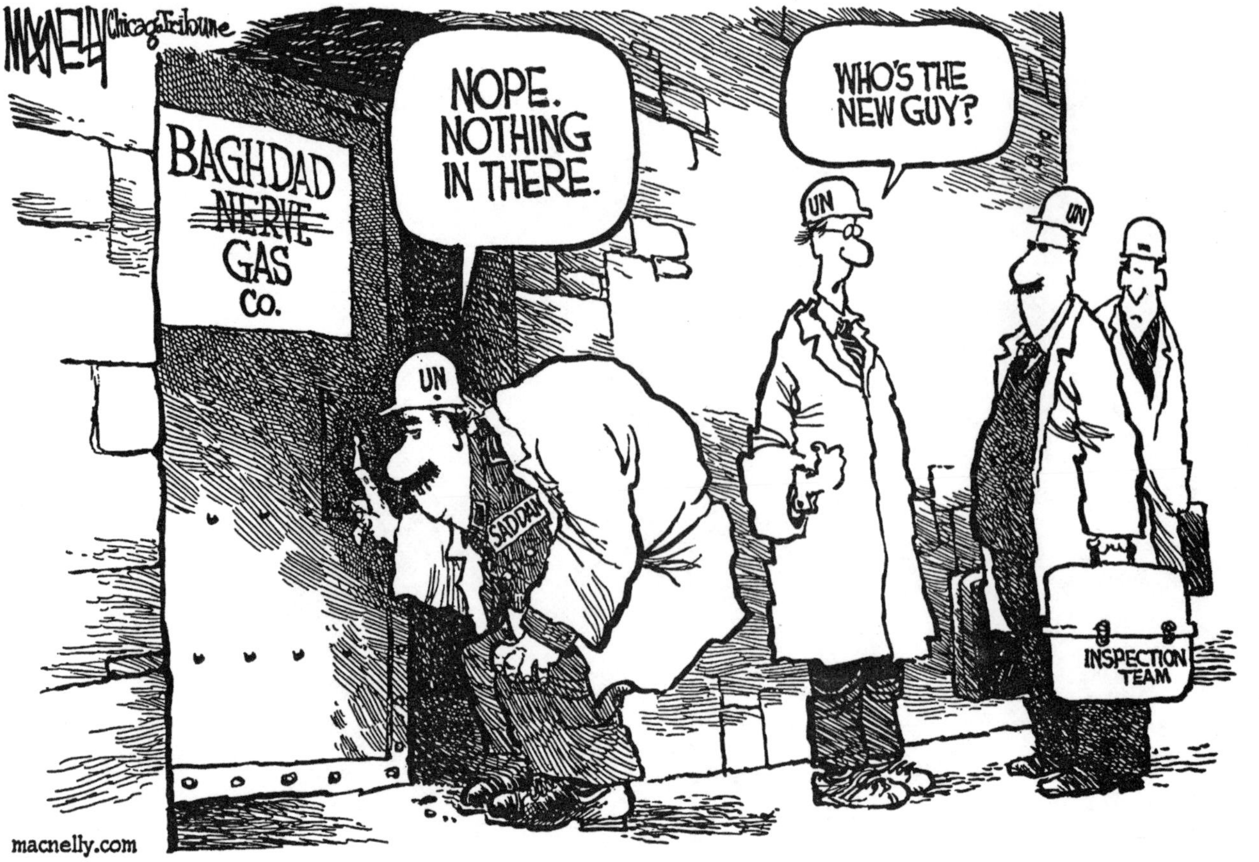
MACNELLY Chicago Tribune
BAGHDAD NERVE GAS CO.
NOPE. NOTHING IN THERE.
WHO'S THE NEW GUY?
UN
SADDAM
INSPECTION TEAM
macnelly.com

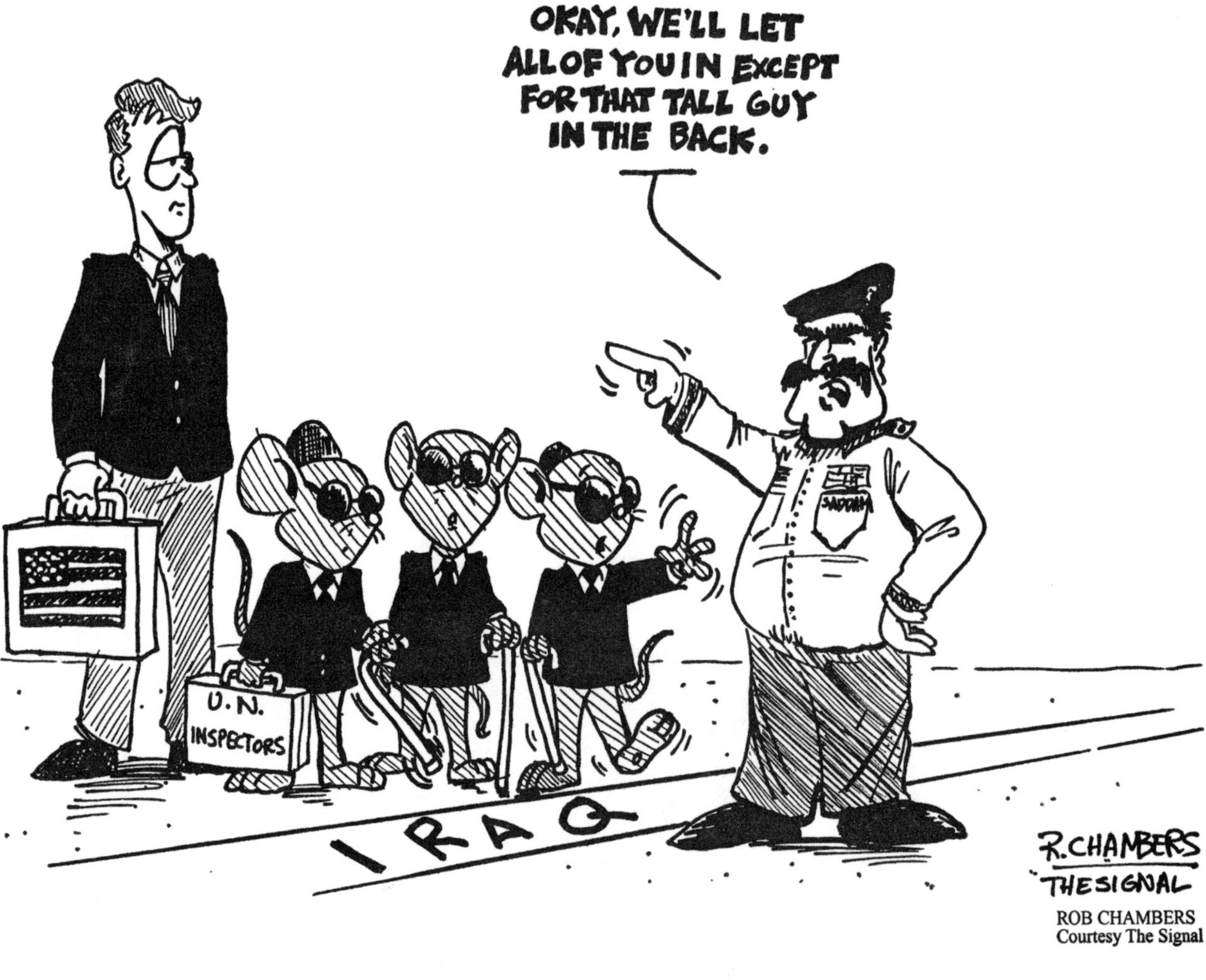
OKAY, WE'LL LET ALL OF YOU IN EXCEPT FOR THAT TALL GUY IN THE BACK.
SADDAM
U.N. INSPECTORS
IRAQ
R.CHAMBERS THE SIGNAL

ROB CHAMBERS
Courtesy The Signal

Foreign Affairs

The United States hesitated in recertifying Mexico for its drug-fighting effort, although Mexican President Ernesto Zedillo insisted that his country was doing everything possible to eliminate drug trafficking within its borders. President Clinton finally approved the recertification and was supported by the U.S. Senate.

The Clinton administration condemned Switzerland for helping Nazi Germany exchange gold plundered from European banks and Holocaust victims. A U.S. government report also criticized U.S. officials for not pressing the Swiss and other neutral countries after the war to return $580 million in looted gold—worth $5.6 billion in today's currency. After a great deal of pressure, Swiss banks began the task of identifying the rightful owners of deposits lost when Jews were slaughtered or forced to leave Germany.

Saddam Hussein tested the world's patience again when he refused to allow American weapons inspectors access to sensitive Iraqi facilities. Iraq is suspected of having developed biological and chemical weapons capable of mass destruction.

South Korea found itself in deep economic trouble following major bankruptcies, and North Korea teetered on the brink of collapse. The U.S. continued to prod Russia to strengthen the security of its nuclear arsenal, and the health of Russian leader Boris Yeltsin was a continuing concern.

GARY MARKSTEIN
Courtesy Milwaukee Journal Sentinel

DANIEL AGUILA
Courtesy Filipino Reporter

LINDA BOILEAU
Courtesy Frankfort State Journal

ROY PETERSON
Courtesy Vancouver Sun

KIRK WALTERS
Courtesy Toledo Blade

MIKE RITTER
Courtesy Tribune Newspapers (Ariz.)

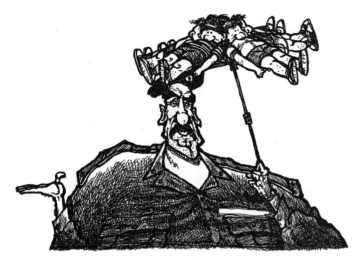

SAD HAPPY DISTRAUGHT HILARIOUS

OUTRAGED SOMBER JOVIAL GRIEF STRICKEN

QUESTION: WHEN WILL THERE BE PEACE IN THE MIDEAST?

ANSWER: WHEN PIGS FLY.

BILL GARNER
Courtesy Washington Times

CLAY BENNETT
Courtesy North American Syndicate

ED GAMBLE
Courtesy Florida Times-Union

DENNY PRITCHARD
Courtesy Toronto Star

JIM BORGMAN
Courtesy Cincinnati Enquirer

ED GAMBLE
Courtesy Florida Times-Union

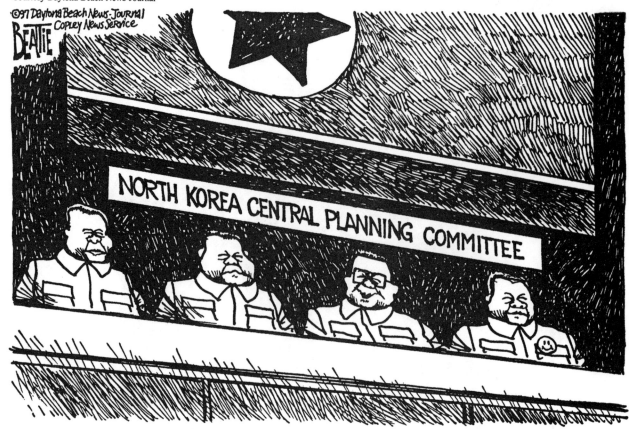

NORTH KOREA CENTRAL PLANNING COMMITTEE

"Look on the bright side. If enough people starve to death, we won't need imperialist American food aid anymore!"

NICK ANDERSON
Courtesy Louisville Courier-Journal

SWISS BANKERS CALCULATE ASSETS TAKEN FROM HOLOCAUST VICTIMS

MIKE PETERS
Courtesy Dayton Daily News

JOHN SHERFFIUS
Courtesy Ventura County Star

MIKE LANE
Courtesy Baltimore Sun

ETTA HULME
Courtesy Fort Worth Star-Telegram

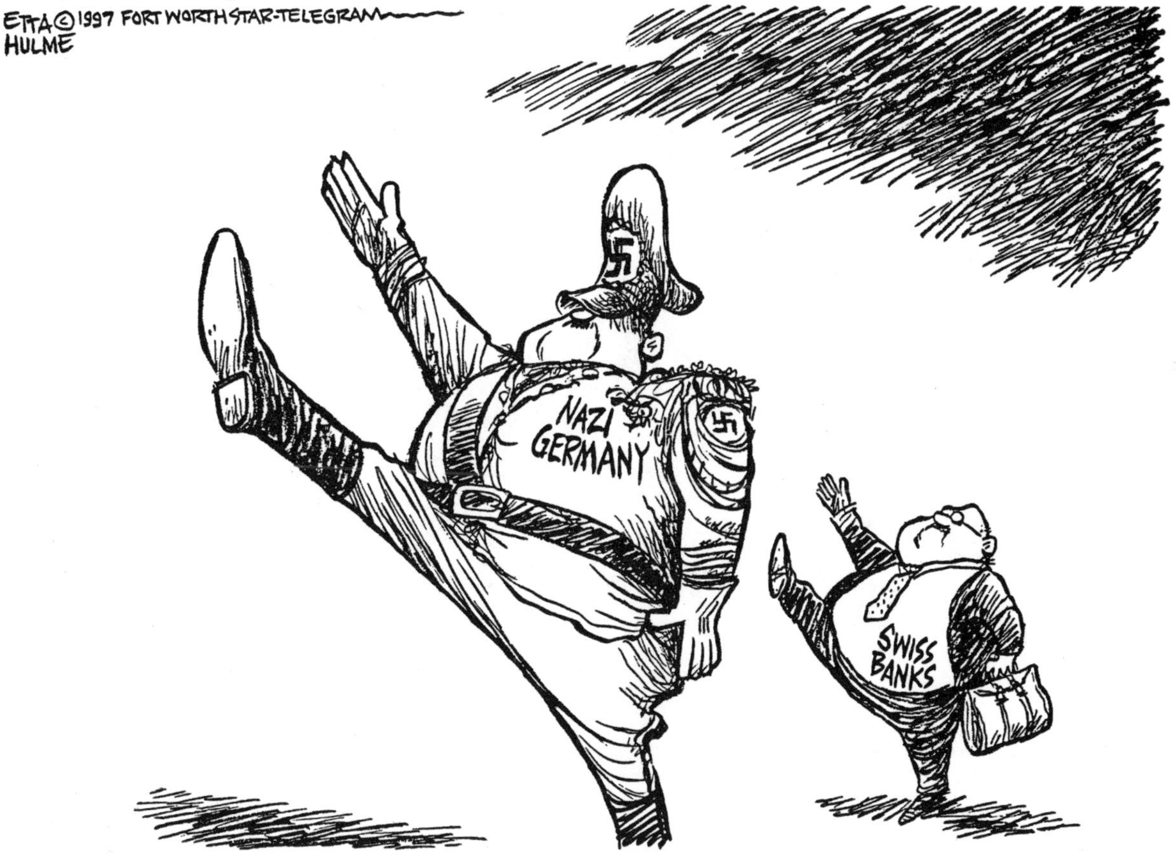
ETTA HULME ©1997 FORT WORTH STAR-TELEGRAM
NAZI GERMANY
SWISS BANKS

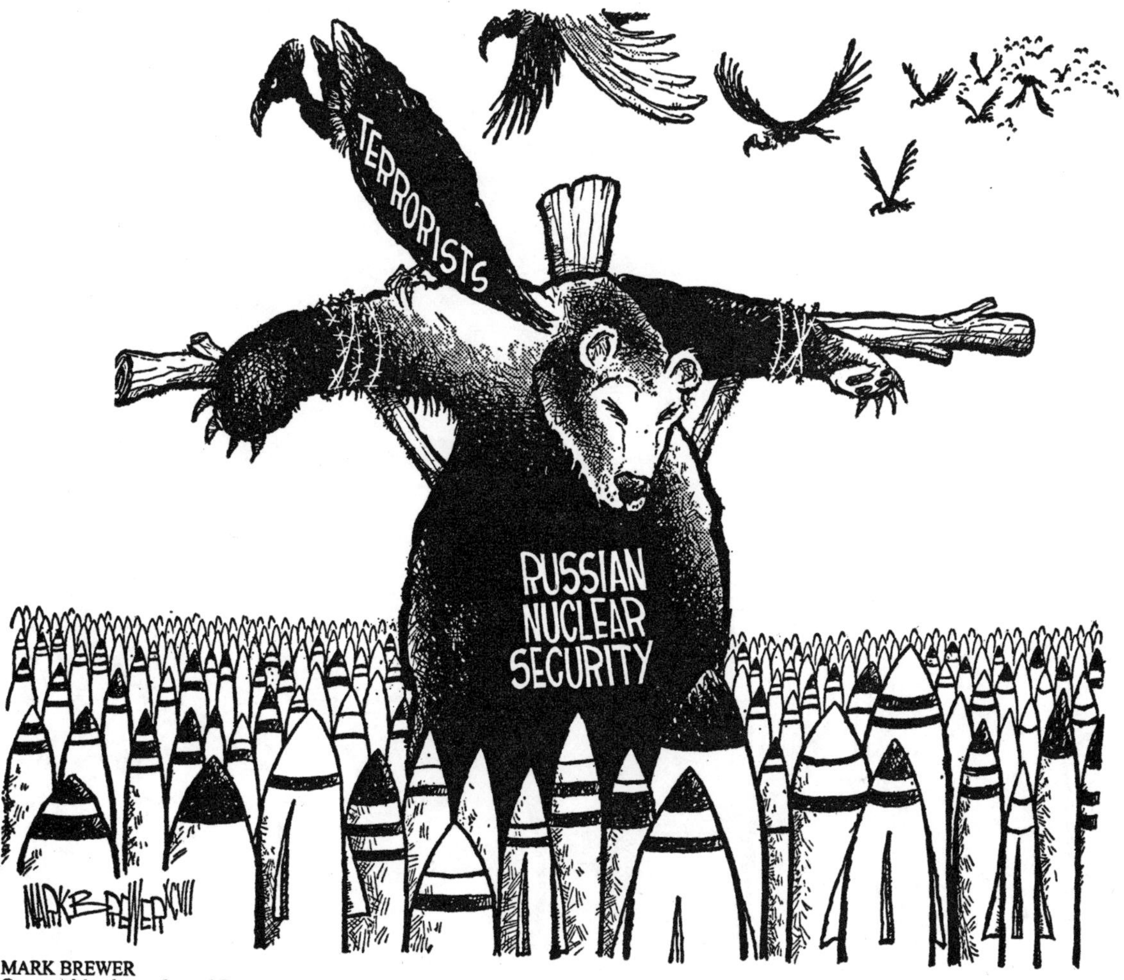
TERRORISTS
RUSSIAN NUCLEAR SECURITY
MARK BREWER XCVII

MARK BREWER
Courtesy Manchester Journal Enquirer

JOHN TREVER
Courtesy Albuquerque Journal

DICK LOCHER
Courtesy Chicago Tribune

54

China

Power in China passed from long-ailing Supreme Leader Deng Xiaoping, who died in February, to his chosen successor, President Jiang Zemin. In a visit to the United States, the new Chinese president was warmly received by President Clinton and by crowds at many planned stops.

Many Americans, however, criticized Zemin's visit, recalling the carnage at Tiananmen Square in Beijing, where Chinese authorities brutally put down growing protests for more individual freedom. Chinese dissident Wei Jingsheng, who was freed from prison, visited the U.S. to urge the release of more political prisoners. In talks with President Zemin, President Clinton urged China to demonstrate more progress in the area of human rights, but Zemin told Clinton, in effect, that it was none of his business.

American companies are not letting the question of human rights deter them from expanding operations in China. Coca Cola, Nike, Ford, and others see the country as a potential gold mine and have moved rapidly to develop business ties.

Hong Kong, which had been a British colony since the end of the Opium War in 1842, reverted to Chinese rule on July 1. Many residents of the city of 6.3 million feared repressive measures, such as the anti-democratic crackdown at Tiananmen Square, might soon follow.

KIRK WALTERS
Courtesy Toledo Blade

©1997 The Toledo Blade
KIRK

JUNKED

JIM LANGE
Courtesy Daily Oklahoman

DESIGN FOR DENG XIAOPING MEMORIAL...

CHRIS OBRION
Courtesy Free Lance-Star (Va.)

JOHN SPENCER
Courtesy Philadelphia Business Journal

WALT HANDELSMAN
Courtesy New Orleans Times-Picayune

DENNIS DRAUGHON
Courtesy Scranton Times

NICK ANDERSON
Courtesy Louisville Courier-Journal

ED GAMBLE
Courtesy Florida Times-Union

JIMMY MARGULIES
Courtesy The Record (N.J.)

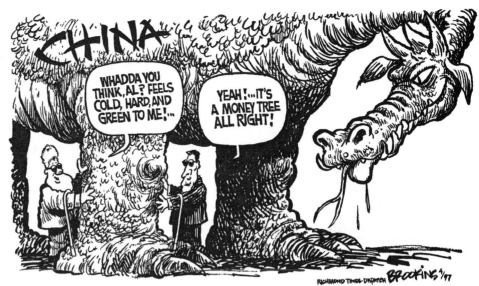

GARY BROOKINS
Courtesy Richmond Times-Dispatch

ED TAYLOR
Courtesy Daily Iowan

CHIP BOK
Courtesy Akron Beacon Journal

59

"Tell me, Senator . . . why are people so cynical about politics in America?"

Congress

Both houses of Congress simultaneously passed money bills intended to produce the first balanced federal budget in a third of a century, while at the same time revamping Medicare, Medicaid, and other major spending programs. The deficit in spending dropped from $90 billion in mid-1997 to less than $22 billion, if administration figures were to be believed. Bouyed by higher tax revenues generated by a growing economy and cuts in spending worked out by Congress and the president, advocates announced that a balanced budget might be achieved three years earlier than anticipated.

Congress spent much of its time wrestling with the thorny problem of campaign finance reform. Republicans preferred to pursue violations of existing laws. Democrats, insisting that "everybody does it," argued that the focus should be on reforming outdated laws. Nevertheless, amid all the arguments over reform, most of the lawmakers were busily collecting money for future campaigns.

In September, Sen. Fred Thompson, a Republican, and Sen. John Glenn, a Democrat, agreed to suspend indefinitely their committee's long investigation of possible White House wrongdoing in fund-raising.

There were heated arguments from both sides over the issue of continued funding for the Endowment of the Arts. Many conservatives in Congress called for an end to funding the program, but it did not happen.

STEVE KELLEY
Courtesy San Diego Union-Tribune

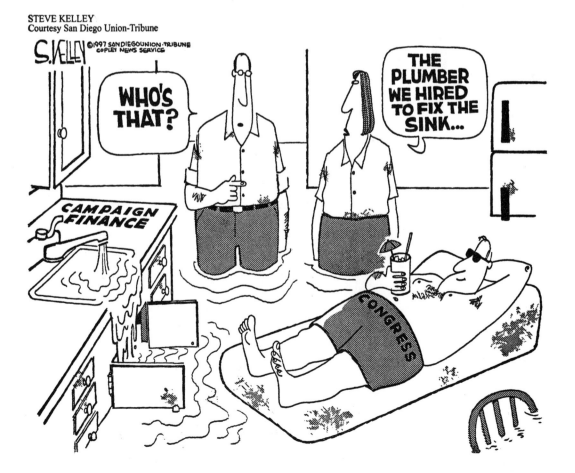

ANN TELNAES
Courtesy Los Angeles Times

JOE RANK
Courtesy Rockford Register-Star

STEPHEN TEMPLETON
Courtesy Comic Relief / Future Feature

DICK LOCHER
Courtesy Chicago Tribune

GEORGE DANBY
Courtesy Bangor Daily News

PETER DUNLAP-SHOHL
Courtesy Anchorage Daily News

YOU THINK GETTING A **CAMEL** THROUGH A NEEDLE'S EYE IS TOUGH...

CHIP BOK
Courtesy Akron Beacon Journal

DICK WRIGHT
Courtesy Columbus Dispatch

S.C. RAWLS
Courtesy Rockdale Citizen

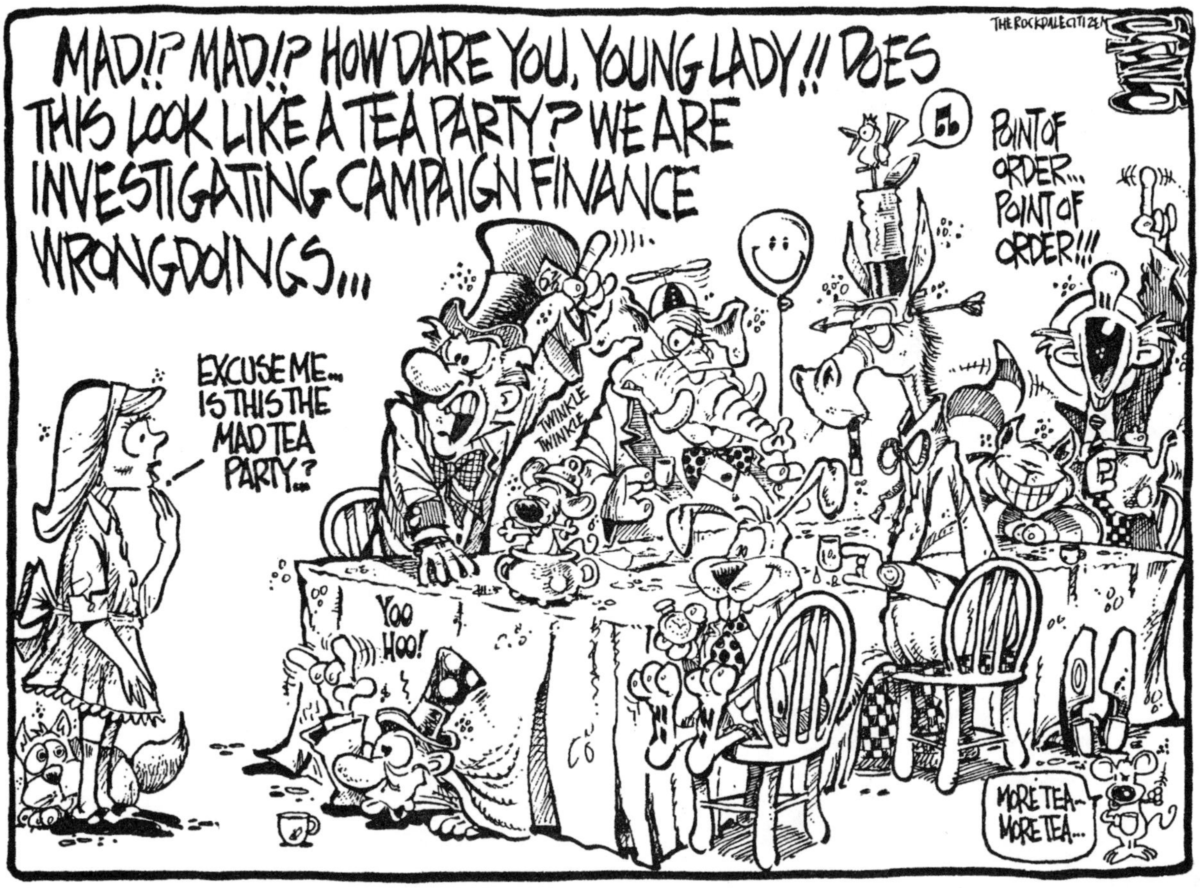
MAD!? MAD!? HOW DARE YOU, YOUNG LADY!! DOES THIS LOOK LIKE A TEA PARTY? WE ARE INVESTIGATING CAMPAIGN FINANCE WRONGDOINGS...
EXCUSE ME... IS THIS THE MAD TEA PARTY...?
POINT OF ORDER... POINT OF ORDER!!!
TWINKLE TWINKLE
YOO HOO!
MORE TEA... MORE TEA...
THE ROCKDALE CITIZEN

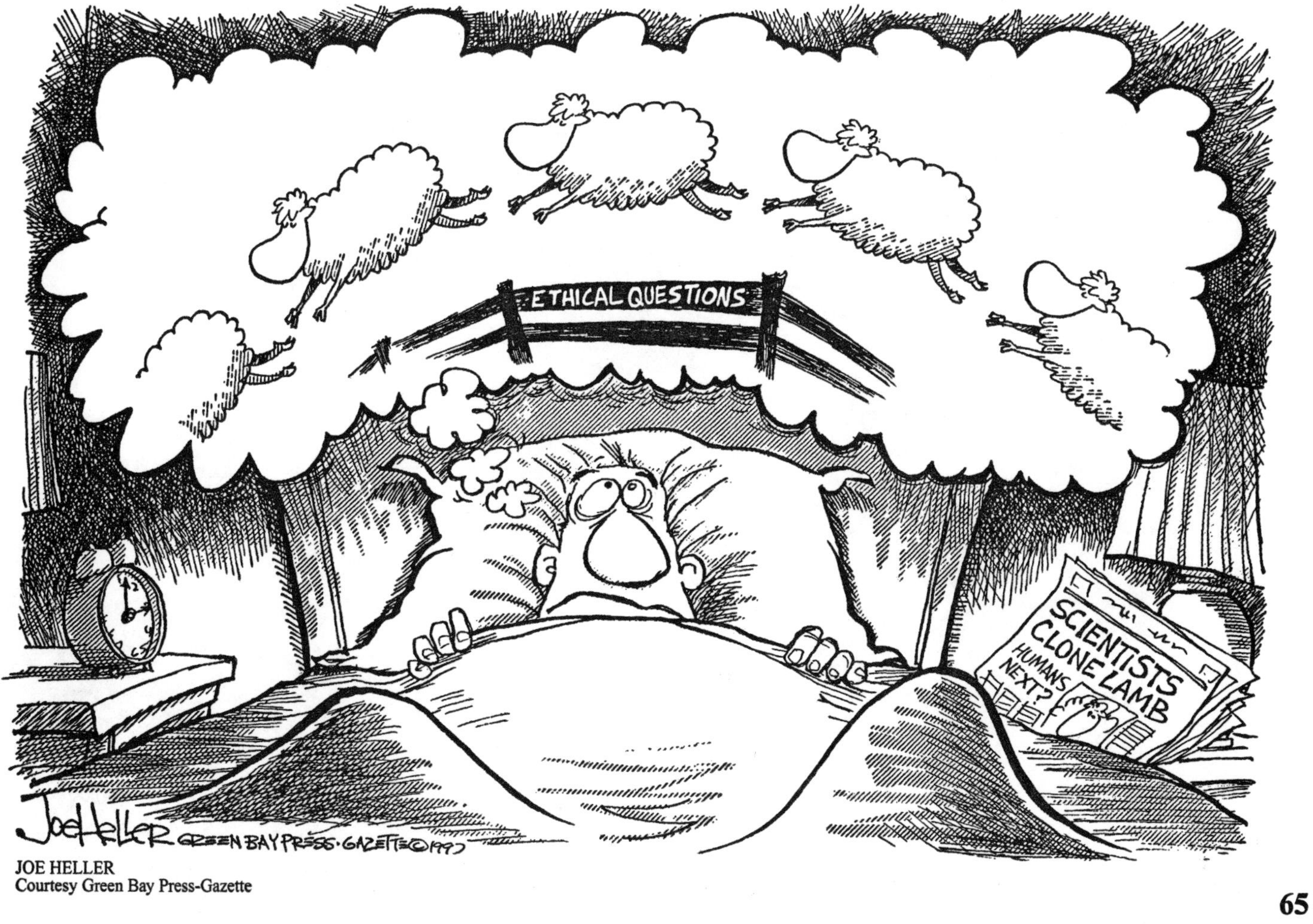
ETHICAL QUESTIONS
SCIENTISTS CLONE LAMB
HUMANS NEXT?
Joe Heller GREEN BAY PRESS-GAZETTE ©1997

JOE HELLER
Courtesy Green Bay Press-Gazette

STEVE SACK
Courtesy Minneapolis Star-Tribune

CLYDE WELLS
Courtesy Augusta Chronicle

TIM BENSON
Courtesy Sioux Falls Argus Leader

CHAN LOWE
Courtesy Fort Lauderdale Sun-Sentinel

NATIONAL ENDOWMENT *for the* **NUTS**

CHIP BECK
Courtesy Political Graphics

DRAPER HILL
Courtesy Detroit News

JIMMY MARGULIES
Courtesy The Record (N.J.)

68

ERIC SMITH
Courtesy Annapolis Capital-Gazette

MIKE LANE
Courtesy Baltimore Sun

BRIAN DUFFY
Courtesy Des Moines Register

ROB ROGERS
Courtesy Pittsburgh Post-Gazette

Politics

Republican House Speaker Newt Gingrich in early 1997 was censured by the House Ethics Committee and fined $300,000. It marked the first time a speaker of the House had ever suffered such an indignity. Gingrich admitted that he had not adequately separated political activities from tax-exempt activities and acknowledged having made unintentional misstatements to ethics investigators. Republican rebels later tried to oust Gingrich as speaker, but the move failed.

A political brush fire broke out when President Clinton nominated Republican William Weld to be ambassador to Mexico. Sen. Jesse Helms held up hearing on the nomination, citing Weld's "soft" views on drugs. Eventually, Weld gave up and withdrew his name from consideration.

Independent counsel Kenneth Starr announced he would step down as head of the investigation of the Whitewater affair to become dean of the law school at Pepperdine University. He had second thoughts, however, and a few days later declared he would press forward with the investigation. Democrats urged Starr to end the probe if he did not produce results soon.

Congress talked a lot about campaign finance reform but made little effort to achieve it. Sen. Fred Thompson's hearings on possible White House violations of the law in raising campaign funds was suspended indefinitely. No one seemed to care.

DICK WRIGHT
Courtesy Columbus Dispatch

JOHN BRANCH
Courtesy San Antonio Express-News

MATT DAVIES
Courtesy Gannett Suburban Newspapers

HANK MCCLURE
Courtesy Lawton Constitution

MARK THORNHILL
Courtesy North County Times (Calif.)

CHRIS OBRION
Courtesy Free Lance-Star (Va.)

MILT PRIGGEE
Courtesy Spokane Spokesman-Review

JOHN BRANCH
Courtesy San Antonio Express-News

BRUMSIC BRANDON, JR.
Courtesy Florida Today

STEVEN LAIT
Courtesy Oakland Tribune

ED STEIN
Courtesy Rocky Mountain News

JEFF KOTERBA
Courtesy Omaha World-Herald

CLYDE WELLS
Courtesy Augusta Chronicle

Berry's World

JIM BERRY
Courtesy NEA

Mr. President, we've got someone Jesse Helms will support as ambassador to Mexico...

KEVIN KALLAUGHER
Courtesy Baltimore Sun

"I SHALL CONTINUE AS INDEPENDENT COUNSEL."

PAUL CONRAD
Courtesy Los Angeles Times Syndicate

GARY MARKSTEIN
Courtesy Milwaukee Journal Sentinel

STEVE GREENBERG
Courtesy Seattle Post-Intelligencer

MIKE THOMPSON
Courtesy State Journal-Register (Ill.)

CHUCK ASAY
Courtesy Colorado Springs Gazette Telegraph

STEVE GREENBERG
Courtesy Seattle Post-Intelligencer

Berry's World

DOING CAMPAIGN-FINANCE REFORM

STEVE MCBRIDE
Courtesy Independence Daily Reporter (Kan.)

KIRK WALTERS
Courtesy Toledo Blade

The Military

The military moved during the year toward a kinder, gentler form of basic training. Drill instructors no longer are given broad discretion on how best to whip recruits into shape. Profanity, touching recruits, and excessive physical requirements are now out. The Pentagon was hit by new charges of sexual harassment in the military. After the Army's highest-ranking enlisted man was brought up on charges, the services began to reexamine their policies of training men and women together. Lt. Kelly Flinn, the Air Force's only female B-52 pilot, accepted a general discharge after she was accused of having an affair with a married man and later lying about it.

Virginia Military Institute began accepting women in 1997. True UFO believers gathered at Roswell, New Mexico, to mark the anniversary of what many claimed was a visit by extraterrestrials fifty years ago. In an attempt to preempt the celebration, Air Force officials held a press conference to announce that bodies reportedly seen by Roswell residents were actually crash dummies.

Following Princess Diana's death, interest grew in one of her stated objectives, the outlawing of land mines. Representatives of 121 nations signed an anti-land mine treaty, but the U.S. refused to do so.

DAVID HITCH
Courtesy Worcester Telegram-Gazette

BOB ENGLEHART
Courtesy Hartford Courant

MALCOLM MAYES
Courtesy Edmonton Journal

JOHN SHERFFIUS
Courtesy Ventura County Star

JAMES MCCLOSKEY
Courtesy Staunton Daily News Leader

JOHN SHERFFIUS
Courtesy Ventura County Star

MINE FIELD

JIM LANGE
Courtesy Daily Oklahoman

J.R. ROSE
Courtesy Byrd Newspapers (Va.)

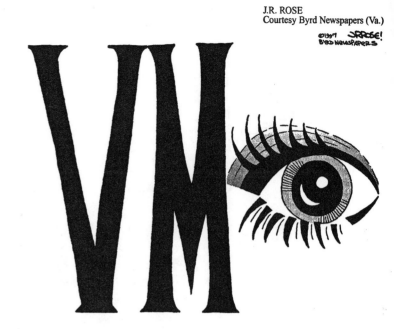

ETTA HULME
Courtesy Fort Worth Star-Telegram

'60s

'90s

JEFF STAHLER
Courtesy Cincinnati Post

JIM BORGMAN
Courtesy Cincinnati Enquirer

BOB GORRELL
Courtesy Richmond Times-Dispatch

NEWS ITEM: MILITARY BASIC TRAINING GOING SOFT...

DAVID GRANLUND
Courtesy Middlesex News (Mass.)

LARRY WRIGHT
Courtesy Detroit News

MIKE LANE
Courtesy Baltimore Sun

ERIC SMITH
Courtesy Annapolis Capital-Gazette

TOM ENGELHARDT
Courtesy St. Louis Post-Dispatch

'. . . And Be Sure To Bring All Your Bank Books, Ledgers
And Investment Records When You Come For The Audit'

BOB LANG
Courtesy The News-Sentinel (Ind.)

The IRS

Hearings by the Senate Finance Committee revealed wide-scale abuse and intimidation of taxpayers by the Internal Revenue Service, as well as instances of corruption in the IRS management. The news came as no great surprise to many Americans. Taxpayers and IRS officials (whose identities were kept secret to prevent retaliation) testified about a system that is driven not by fairness but by quotas. Witnesses testified that managers were sometimes pressured to handle as many cases as possible and to collect as much money from taxpayers as possible. IRS employees said that officers of the agency were taught that all taxpayers were cheating the government. At the same time, one witness claimed, the "climate and culture" of the IRS hindered any investigation of the agency's wrongdoing.

Dealing with the IRS in 1998 could be a bit less arduous for many people, but things are not expected to change much. The reforms worked out by the White House and Congress still will not make tax forms more understandable. Intrusive audits, however, which in the past allowed curious agents to check out such mundane facts as what model car a person drives, will be curtailed. In addition, taking the IRS to court in modest disputes will be easier than before.

GARY BROOKINS
Courtesy Richmond Times-Dispatch

91

S. Lait

I NEED TO SEE YOUR TAX RETURNS AND RECEIPTS FOR THE PAST FIVE YEARS...

IRS

STEVEN LAIT
Courtesy Oakland Tribune

IRS

HK MERCADO '97

"THE TAX PAYERS"

JAMES MERCADO
Courtesy Honolulu Advertiser

HANK MCCLURE
Courtesy Lawton Constitution

HOUSE

OVERHAUL TIME!

IRS

Hank

THE NEW 'IMPROVED' I.R.S.

GLENN MCCOY
Courtesy Belleville News-Democrat

DOUGLAS REGALIA
Courtesy San Ramon Valley Times

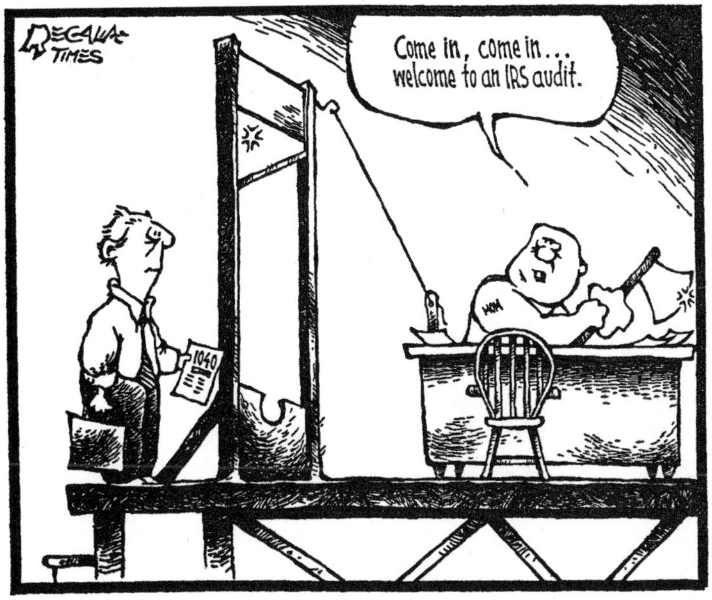
Come in, come in... welcome to an IRS audit.
1040
REGALIA TIMES

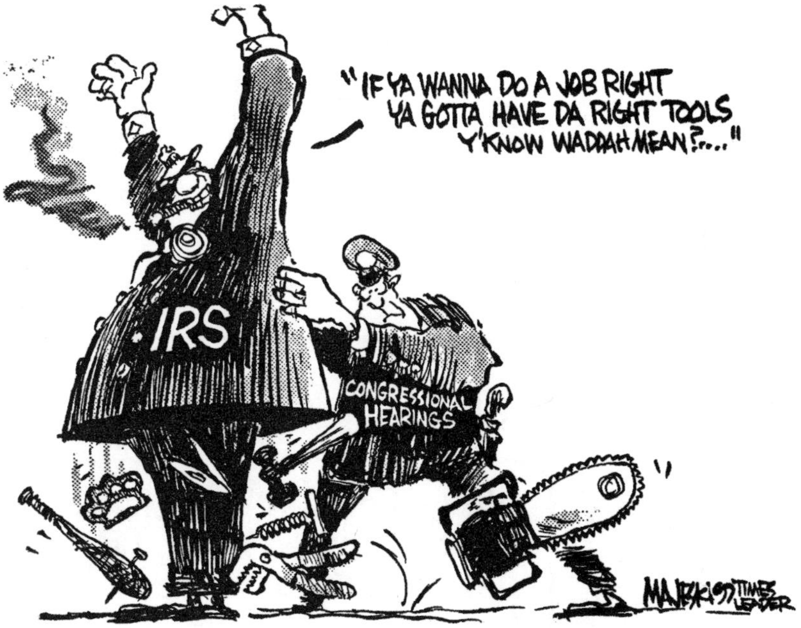
"IF YA WANNA DO A JOB RIGHT YA GOTTA HAVE DA RIGHT TOOLS Y'KNOW WADDAHMEAN?..."
IRS
CONGRESSIONAL HEARINGS

JOE MAJESKI
Courtesy The Times Leader (Pa.)

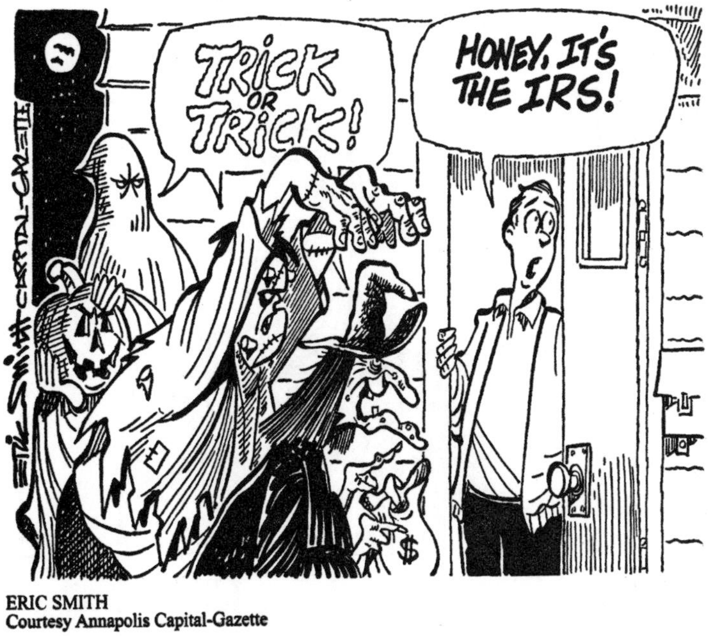
TRICK OR TRICK!
HONEY, IT'S THE IRS!

ERIC SMITH
Courtesy Annapolis Capital-Gazette

CLAY JONES
Courtesy Honolulu Star-Bulletin

SCOTT NICKEL
Courtesy Antelope Valley Press

WAYNE STAYSKAL
Courtesy Tampa Tribune

CHAN LOWE
Courtesy Fort Lauderdale Sun-Sentinel

AARON TAYLOR
Courtesy Deseret News (Utah)

JIM JORDAN
Courtesy Elmhurst Press (Ill.)

Society

Princess Diana's fatal automobile wreck initially was blamed on a horde of pursuing paparazzi, the celebrity photographers who frequently followed her. Later it was determined by authorities that the driver of the Mercedes in which she was riding was legally drunk.

Southern Baptists called for a boycott of the Disney Corporation to protest the company's apparent endorsement of gay-lesbian positions, and several hundred thousand Christian men calling themselves the "Promise Keepers" gathered in prayer at the mall in Washington. The movement calls upon men to keep their promises to wives and families and to strive to become better husbands and fathers. Later in the year, the Million Woman March was held in Washington, a response by black women to an earlier Million Man March.

President Clinton belatedly endorsed the widely criticized remarks made by former vice-president Dan Quayle a few years ago when he emphasized the need for children to have a stable family life, with both parents living in the home. A television character named Ellen made news when she came out of the closet and told the world she was a lesbian.

An Iowa woman, Bobbi McCaughey, gave birth to the world's only surviving septuplets after taking fertility drugs, and a 63-year-old woman became the oldest new mother on record.

Congress continued to wrestle with two major problems: how to fix an immigration policy that is clearly flawed, and how to deny children access to unsuitable material on the internet.

CHIP BOK
Courtesy Akron Beacon Journal

"GET BACK IN THE KITCHEN WHERE YOU BELONG!"

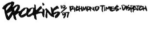

JERRY BARNETT
Courtesy Indianapolis News

ROB ROGERS
Courtesy Pittsburgh Post-Gazette

DON LANDGREN, JR.
Courtesy The Landmark (Mass.)

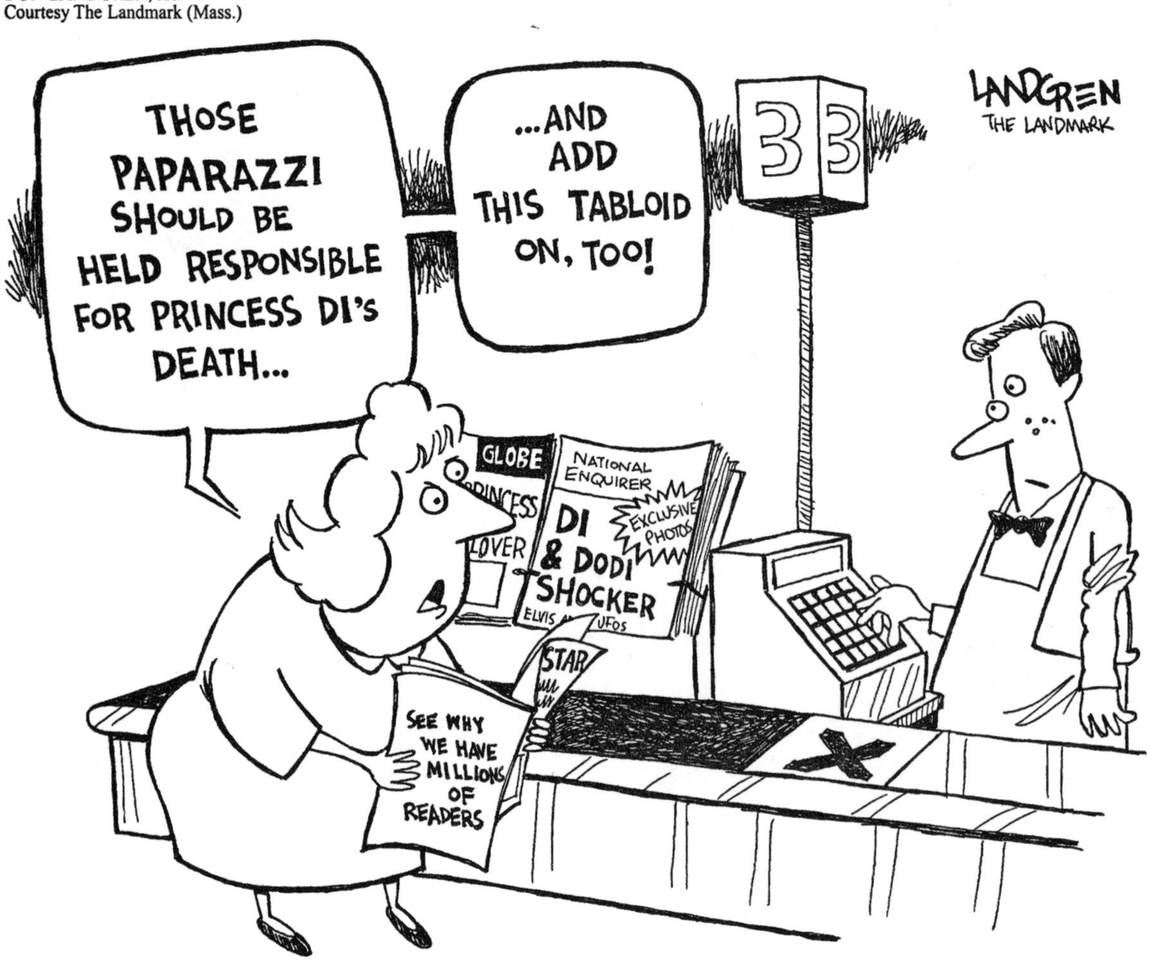
THOSE PAPARAZZI SHOULD BE HELD RESPONSIBLE FOR PRINCESS DI'S DEATH...
...AND ADD THIS TABLOID ON, TOO!
33
LANDGREN
THE LANDMARK
GLOBE
LOVER
NATIONAL ENQUIRER
DI & DODI SHOCKER
EXCLUSIVE PHOTOS
STAR
SEE WHY WE HAVE MILLIONS OF READERS

JOHN MARSHALL
Courtesy Binghampton Press and Sun-Bulletin

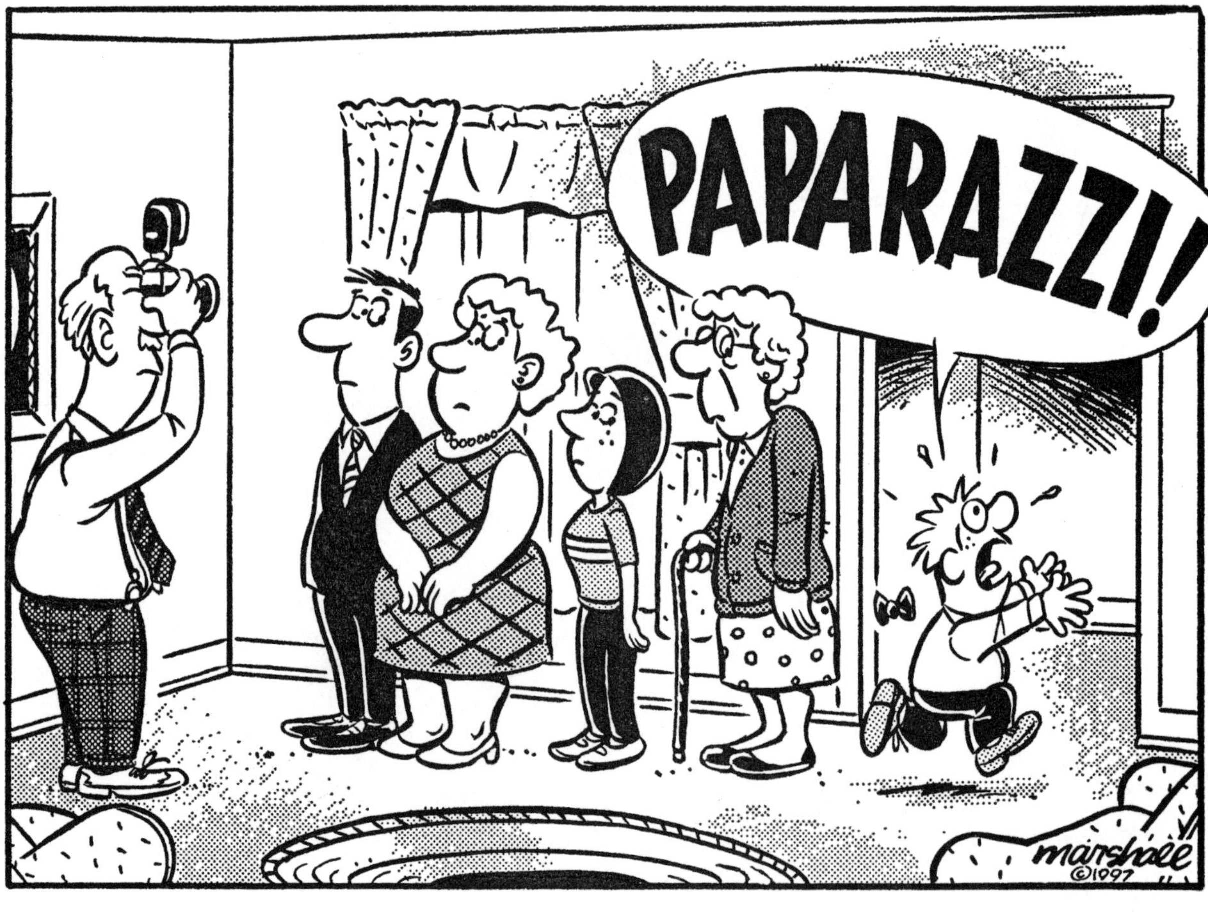
PAPARAZZI!
marshall
©1997

TV 'COMEDY'

CLYDE WELLS
Courtesy Augusta Chronicle

MIKE SMITH
Courtesy United Features Syndicate

ANN CLEAVES
Courtesy Palisadian Post

JOHN SPENCER
Courtesy Philadelphia Business Journal

DAVE SATTLER
Courtesy Lafayette Journal-Courier

ED FISCHER
© 1997 Rochester Post-Bulletin Co.
LLC, Ed Fischer Syndicate
fischer@postbulletin.com

ED FISCHER
Courtesy Rochester Post-Bulletin

MATT DAVIES
Courtesy Gannett Suburban Newspapers

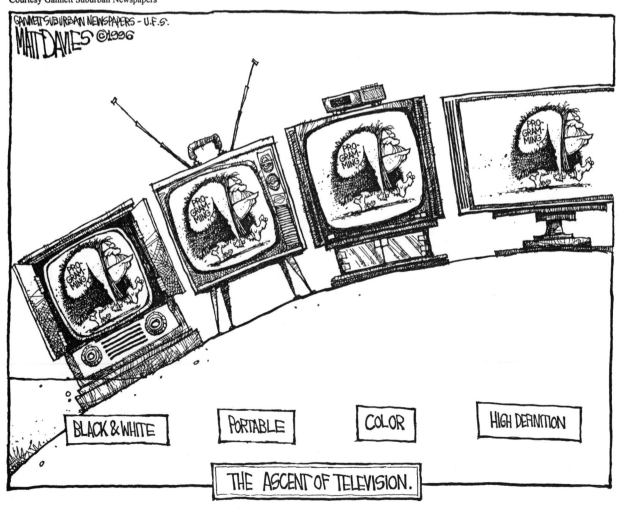

103

CLAY BENNETT
Courtesy North American Syndicate

The Bridge to the 21st Century

CHESTER COMMODORE
Courtesy Chicago Defender

MIKE SMITH
Courtesy United Features Syndicate

RANDY BISH
Courtesy Greensburg Tribune-Review (Pa.)

JEFF MACNELLY
Courtesy Chicago Tribune
and Tribune Media Services

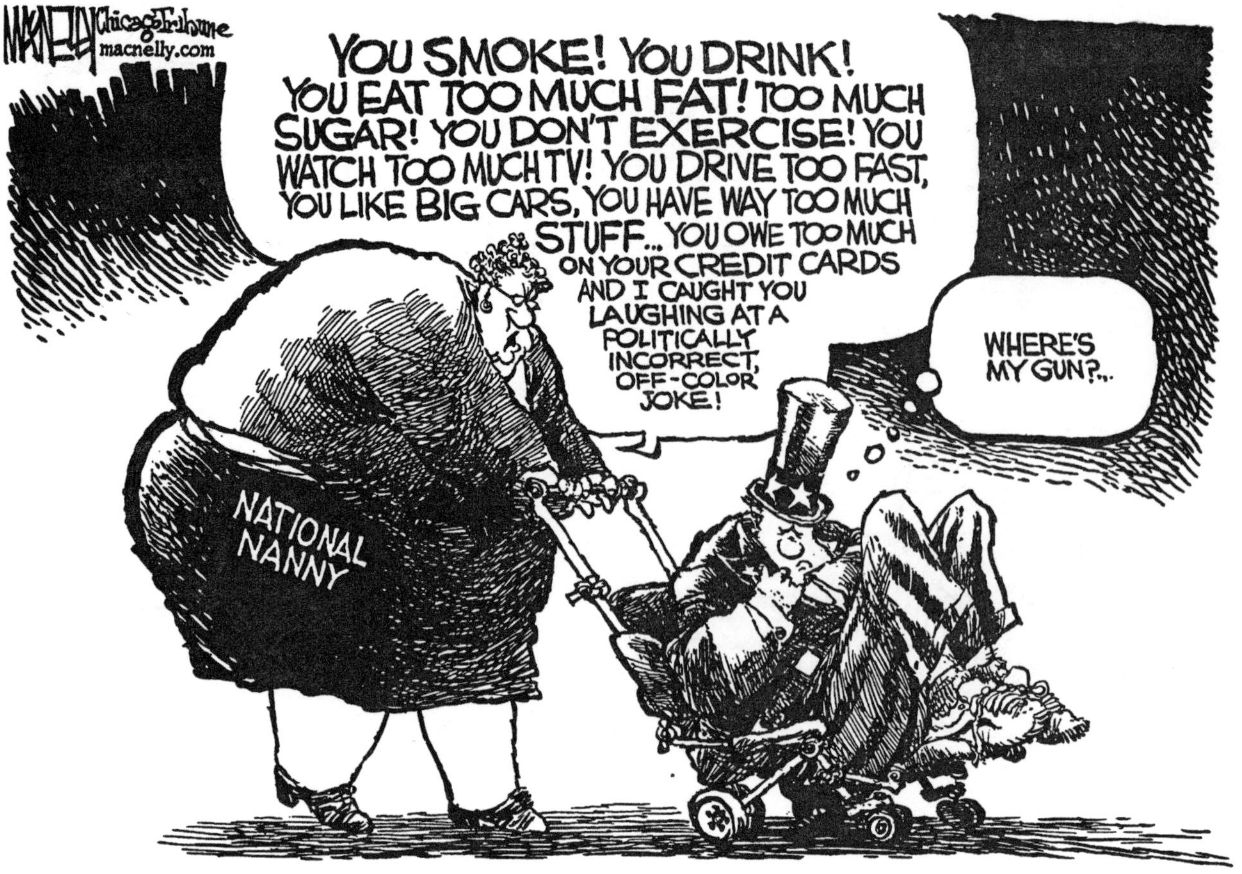
MacNELLY Chicago Tribune macnelly.com
YOU SMOKE! YOU DRINK! YOU EAT TOO MUCH FAT! TOO MUCH SUGAR! YOU DON'T EXERCISE! YOU WATCH TOO MUCH TV! YOU DRIVE TOO FAST, YOU LIKE BIG CARS, YOU HAVE WAY TOO MUCH STUFF... YOU OWE TOO MUCH ON YOUR CREDIT CARDS AND I CAUGHT YOU LAUGHING AT A POLITICALLY INCORRECT, OFF-COLOR JOKE!
WHERE'S MY GUN?..
NATIONAL NANNY

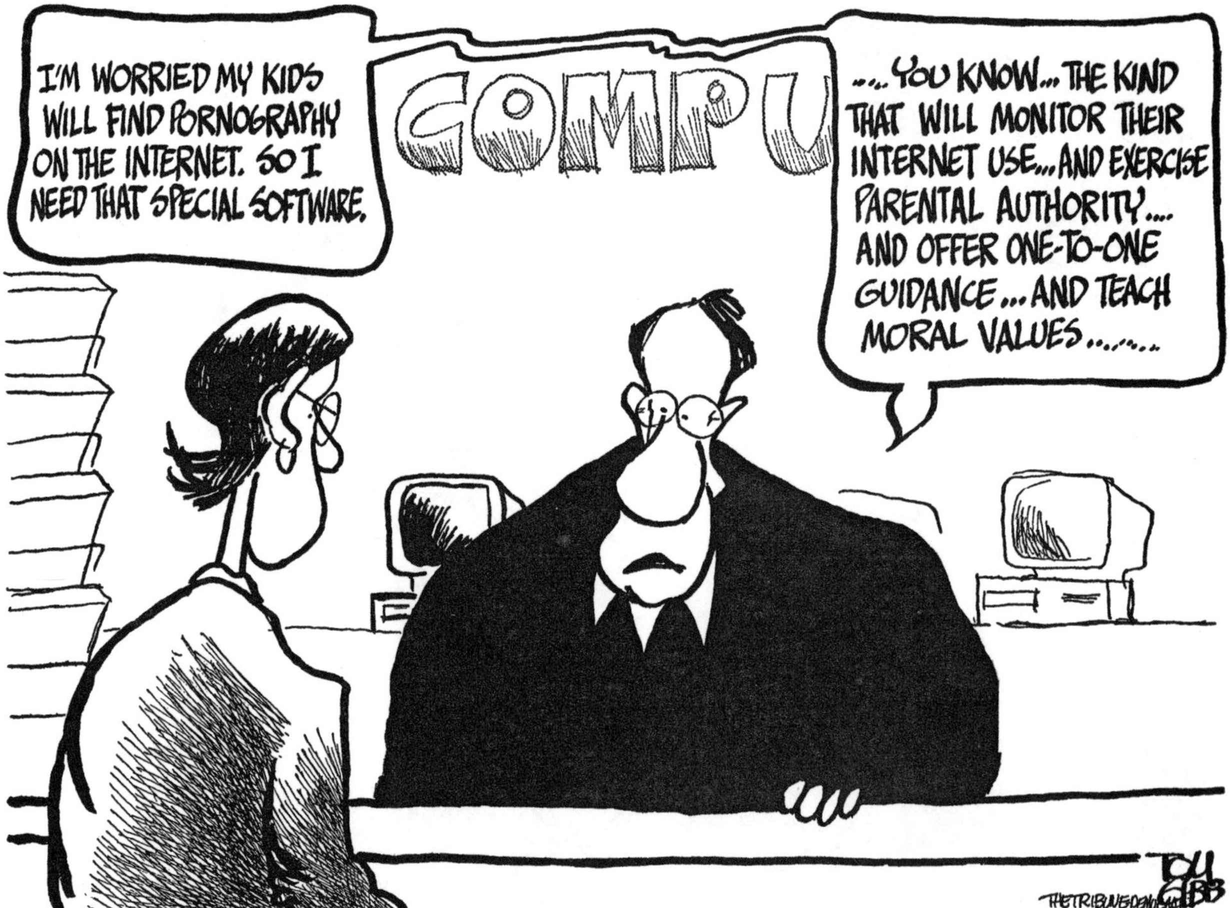
I'M WORRIED MY KIDS WILL FIND PORNOGRAPHY ON THE INTERNET. SO I NEED THAT SPECIAL SOFTWARE.
COMPU
...YOU KNOW... THE KIND THAT WILL MONITOR THEIR INTERNET USE... AND EXERCISE PARENTAL AUTHORITY.... AND OFFER ONE-TO-ONE GUIDANCE... AND TEACH MORAL VALUES.......

TOM GIBB
Courtesy Altoona Tribune-Democrat

DOUG MACGREGOR
Courtesy Fort Myers News-Press

DAVID GRANLUND
Courtesy Middlesex News (Mass.)

CLYDE WELLS
Courtesy Augusta Chronicle

CHARLIE DANIEL
Courtesy Knoxville News-Sentinel

JEFF LITTLE
Courtesy Erie Morning News

MARK BREWER
Courtesy Manchester Journal Enquirer

CHILD WELFARE SYSTEM

NOW

PROMISE KEEPERS

MIKE RITTER
Courtesy Tribune Newspapers (Ariz.)

THUMP

ON WHOM SHALL WE PASS JUDGEMENT TODAY... MARRIED MOTHERS WHO WORK OR UNMARRIED MOTHERS WHO DON'T WORK?

MIKE KEEFE THE DENVER POST 97
MIKE KEEFE
Courtesy Denver Post

RICHARD CROWSON
Courtesy Wichita Eagle

ETTA HULME
Courtesy Fort Worth Star-Telegram

DAVE SATTLER
Courtesy Lafayette Journal-Courier

I'M NOT SURE EVERYONE IS IN AGREEMENT ON THIS DISNEY BOYCOTT THING.

WALT HANDELSMAN
Courtesy New Orleans Times-Picayune

BOB DORNFRIED
Courtesy Wilton Villager

STEVE BREEN
Courtesy Asbury Park Press

ART HENRIKSON
Courtesy Des Plaines Daily Herald

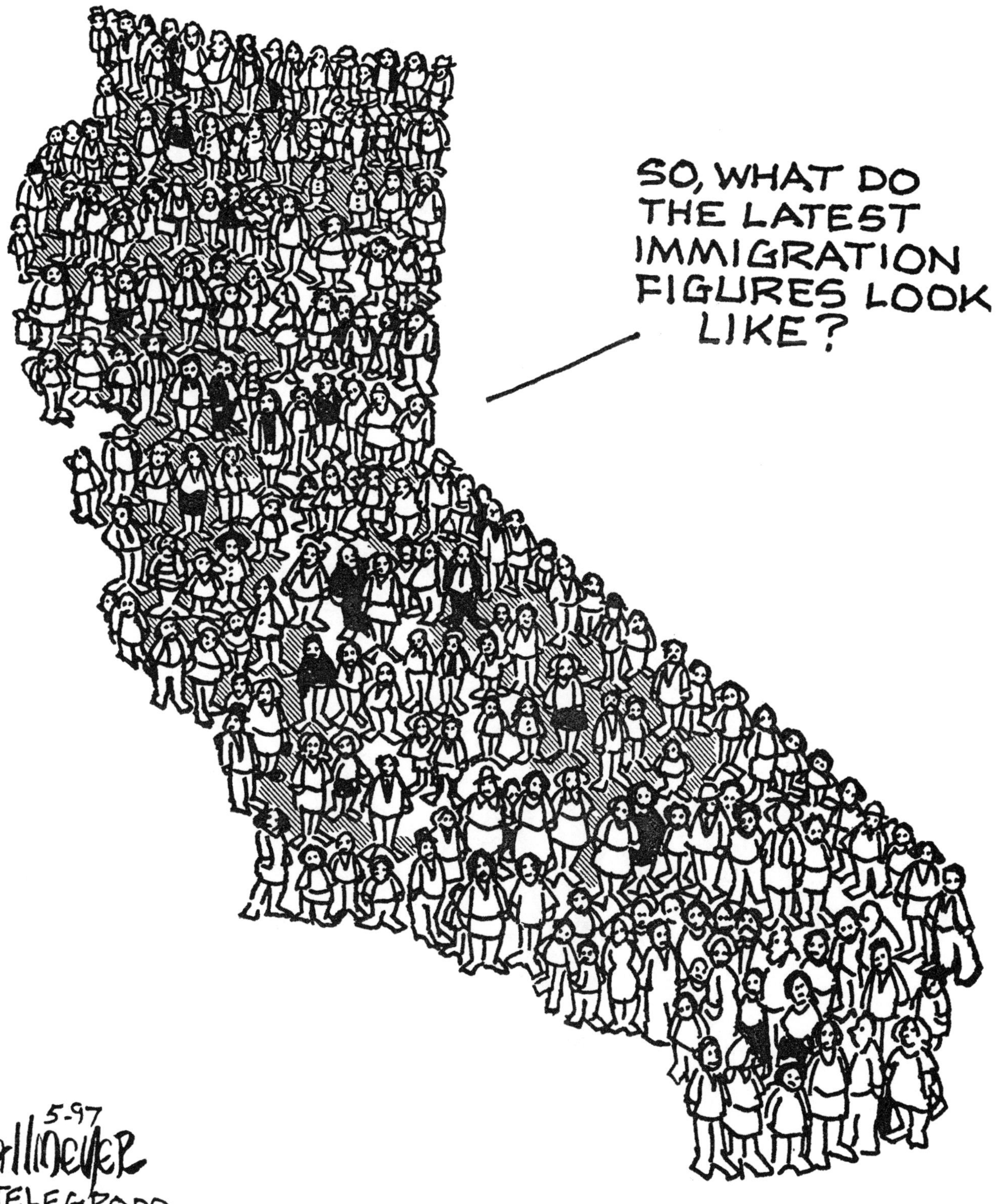
SO, WHAT DO THE LATEST IMMIGRATION FIGURES LOOK LIKE?
5-97
Wallmeyer
PRESS-TELEGRAM

RICHARD WALLMEYER
Courtesy Long Beach Press-Telegram

MARK THORNHILL
Courtesy North County Times (Calif.)

ANNETTE BALESTERI
Courtesy Antioch Ledger-Dispatch (Calif.)

Education

Controversy arose over an Oakland, California, school board's policy recognizing something called black English, or "ebonics," as a separate language used by black students and genetically linked to African speech patterns. Critics claimed that the action would endorse substandard English.

The school board later backtracked, dropping the claim that "ebonics" is genetically based and rescinding an order to teach students both ebonics and standard English.

Early in the year, President Clinton called for "a national crusade for educational standards," proposing a multi-million-dollar program to help youngsters learn to read. He later abandoned the idea of tinkering with standards and focused instead on national testing. His new approach seemed to be in trouble because it was widely regarded as an intrusion of the federal government into local education matters.

Many schools have made student uniforms mandatory, hoping to prevent poor children from being embarrassed by their non-designer clothing. Test scores continued to decline in public schools, and campus violence has yet to be brought under control. Gangs, identified as being responsible for most school shootings, have been in evidence in cities both large and small.

STEVE BREEN
Courtesy Asbury Park Press

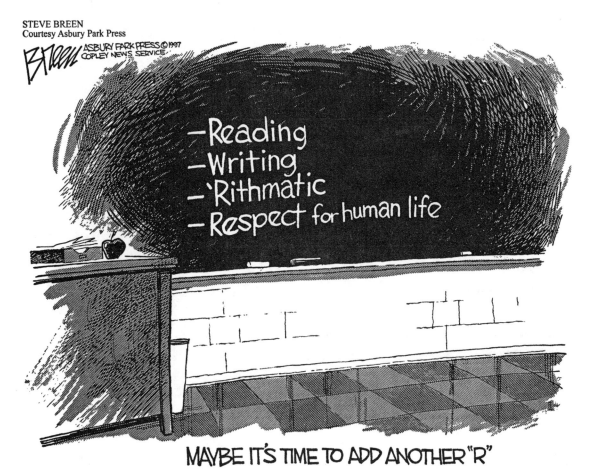

MAYBE IT'S TIME TO ADD ANOTHER "R"

TOM ENGELHARDT
Courtesy St. Louis Post-Dispatch

BILL WHITEHEAD
Courtesy Kansas City Business Journal

'Looks As If We're Stuck — Business Dismantled Most Of It
To Prop Up The Bottom Line'

TIM HARTMAN
Courtesy North Hills New Record (Pa.)

PATRICK ALAN RICE
Courtesy Jupiter Courier

WAYNE STAYSKAL
Courtesy Tampa Tribune

DON LANDGREN, JR.
Courtesy The Landmark (Mass.)

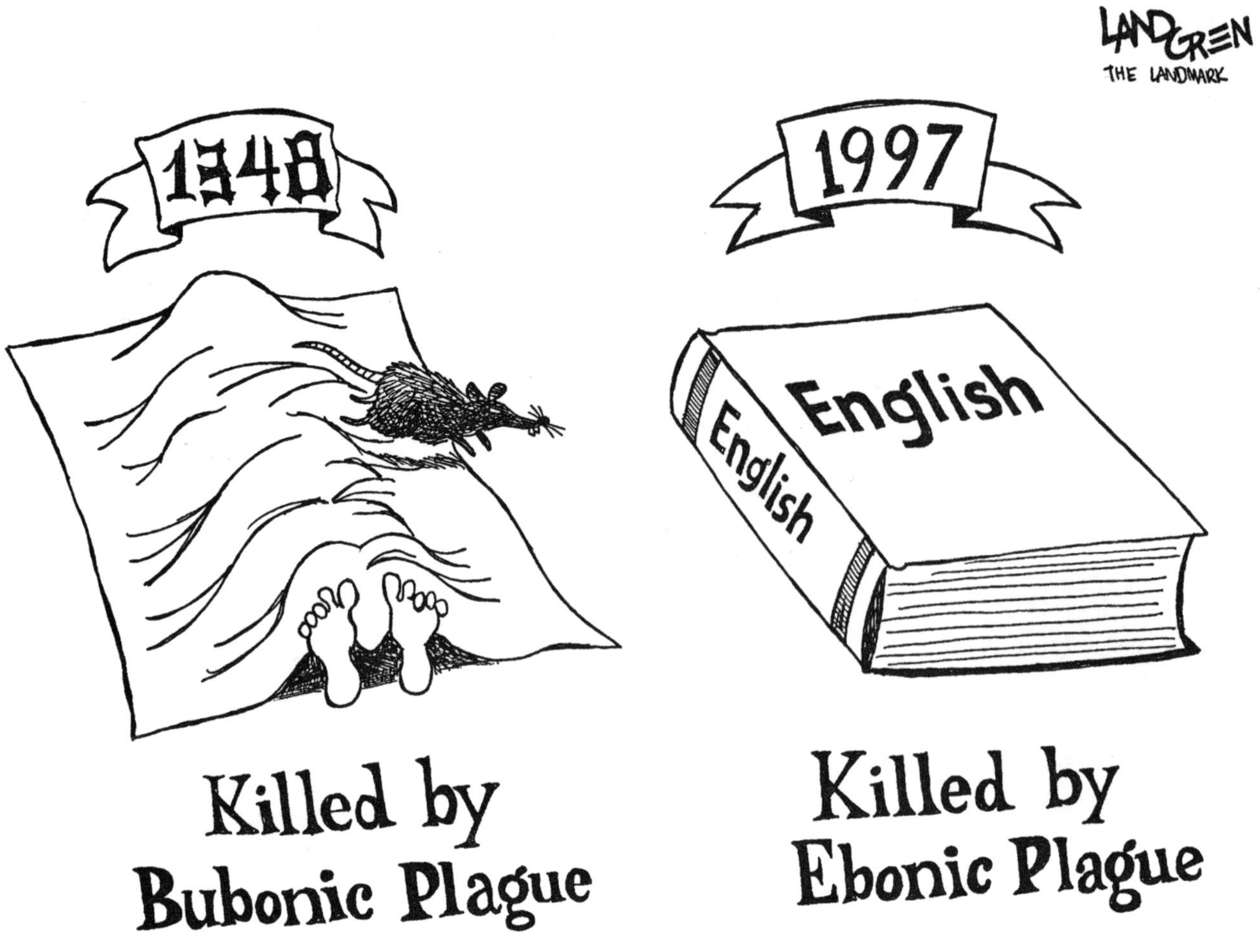
LANDGREN
THE LANDMARK
1348
1997
English
English
Killed by
Bubonic Plague
Killed by
Ebonic Plague

NEIL GRAHAME
Courtesy Spencer Newspapers

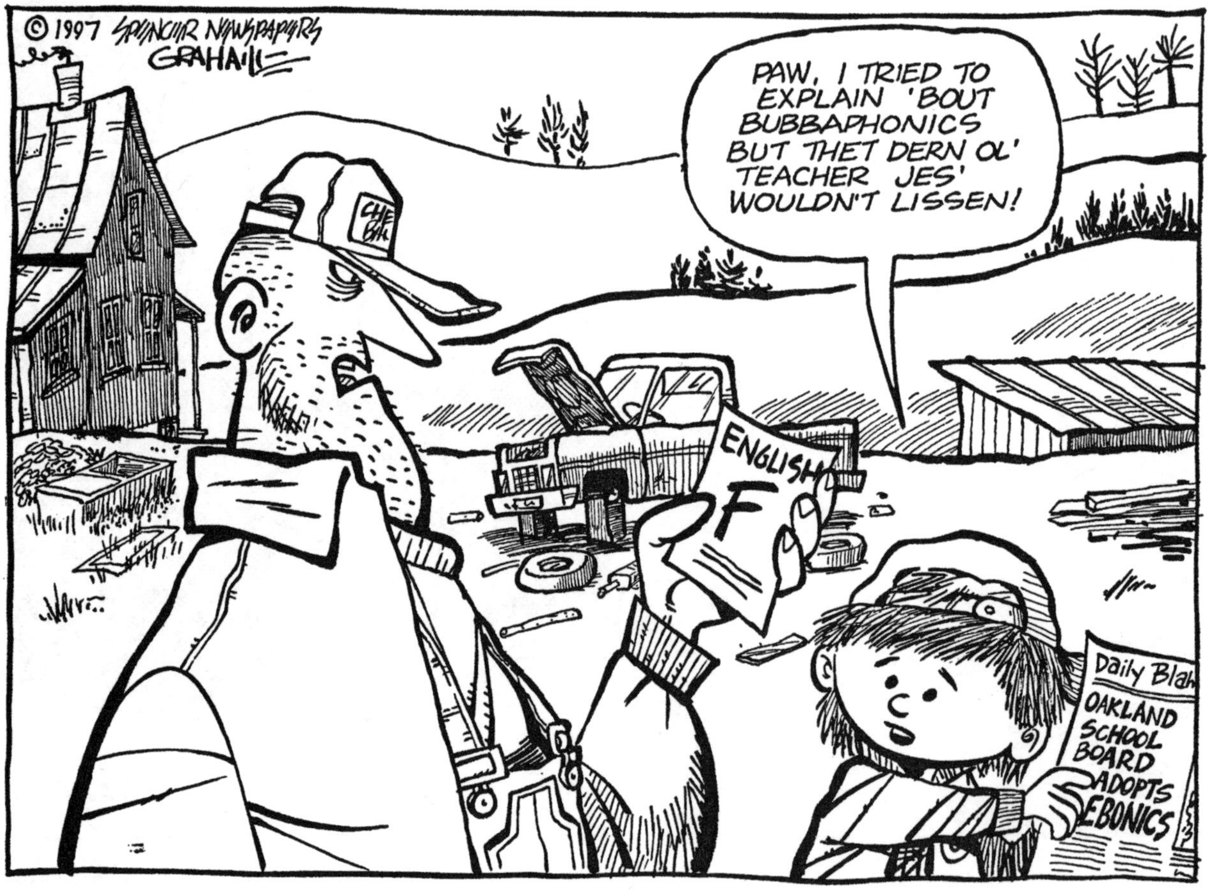
© 1997 SPENCER NEWSPAPERS
GRAHAME
PAW, I TRIED TO EXPLAIN 'BOUT BUBBAPHONICS BUT THET DERN OL' TEACHER JES' WOULDN'T LISSEN!
ENGLISH
F
Daily Blah
OAKLAND SCHOOL BOARD ADOPTS EBONICS

WAYNE STAYSKAL
Courtesy Tampa Tribune

VIC CANTONE
Courtesy King Features / North American Syndicate

PAUL DUGINSKI
Courtesy Los Angeles Times

SCOTT STANTIS
Courtesy Birmingham News

SCOTT STANTIS
Courtesy Birmingham News

DREW SHENEMAN
Courtesy Oakland Press

JOHN TREVER
Courtesy Albuquerque Journal

PAUL FELL
Courtesy Lincoln Journal Star

STACY CURTIS
Courtesy MSNBC & The Times (Ind.)

Crime

Timothy McVeigh was found guilty and sentenced to death in the 1995 Oklahoma City bombing that killed 168 and injured more than 500. Terry Nichols, who was at home with his family in Kansas when the bomb exploded, was convicted of conspiracy and involuntary manslaughter in the tragic attack.

A British au pair, Louise Woodward, was convicted of second-degree murder in the death of an infant who was in her care. The case attracted international attention—and a great deal of criticism. Judge Hiller B. Zobel reduced the jury's verdict to manslaughter and sentenced Woodward to time already served. The baby, Matthew Eappen, was eight months old.

During the year, more than one newborn baby was abandoned by its mother, starkly underscoring the limited value of a life in the minds of some young people today.

School shootings and gang rampages continued throughout 1997. In Kentucky, fourteen-year-old Michael Carneal allegedly sprayed a high school hallway with semiautomatic pistol fire, killing three teenage girls and wounding five other students. Violence, of course, continued unabated on television, as an industry striving for realism made it even more appalling.

DICK LOCHER
Courtesy Chicago Tribune

'STAY TUNED FOR THE PRESIDENT'S PLAN TARGETING PEACE IN IRELAND AND BOSNIA.'

ANN CLEAVES
Courtesy Palisadian Post

ALAN VITELLO
Courtesy Loveland Daily Reporter-Herald (Colo.)

PATRICK ALAN RICE
Courtesy Jupiter Courier

124

JOHN BRANCH
Courtesy San Antonio Express-News

STILL STANDING...

AMERICAN JUSTICE SYSTEM

RICHARD CROWSON
Courtesy Wichita Eagle

CLAY BENNETT
Courtesy North American Syndicate

Volunteers needed to clean up the work of vandals...

JEFF DANZIGER
Courtesy Los Angeles Times Syndicate

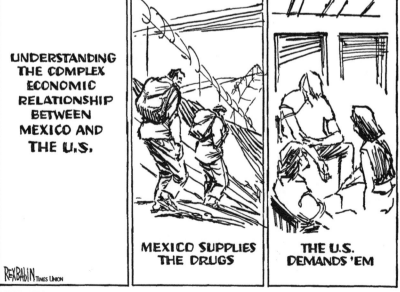

REX BABIN
Courtesy Albany Times Union

WILLIAM L. FLINT
Courtesy Arlington Morning News

MIKE LUCKOVICH
Courtesy Atlanta Constitution

JEFF KOTERBA
Courtesy Omaha World-Herald

AFTER-BIRTH ABORTION

JOHN SPENCER
Courtesy Philadelphia Business Journal

WAYNE STAYSKAL
Courtesy Tampa Tribune

MIKE LUCKOVICH
Courtesy Atlanta Constitution

KEVIN KALLAUGHER
Courtesy Baltimore Sun

The Environment

The debate over global warming continued in talks in Kyoto, Japan. Some Americans complained that the treaty being proposed to deal with global warming was unfair because it exempted most developing countries of the Third World while placing energy restrictions on thirty-four wealthier countries, including the United States and western Europe.

The Clinton administration, however, signaled that the U.S. would be flexible on the matter, and the treaty was approved by delegates from 150 nations. Republican critics denounced the pact and predicted that it would never be ratified by the U.S. Senate.

Weather-wise, 1997 opened on a fierce note. Snowstorms blanketed the Northwest, followed by a thaw and heavy rains that led to mud-slides and flooding, forcing thousands from their homes. Much of the bad weather, plus wild fires in Australia, was blamed on the El Nino phenomenon—warm water in the Pacific Ocean that creates a strong, easterly flow of winds. The phenomenon historically has caused storms in California while minimizing the threat of hurricanes in the east.

Big-city pollution remains a major problem, as researchers strive to develop cleaner-burning gasoline for automobiles. In addition, cities have begun to enforce smoke-abatement laws more vigorously.

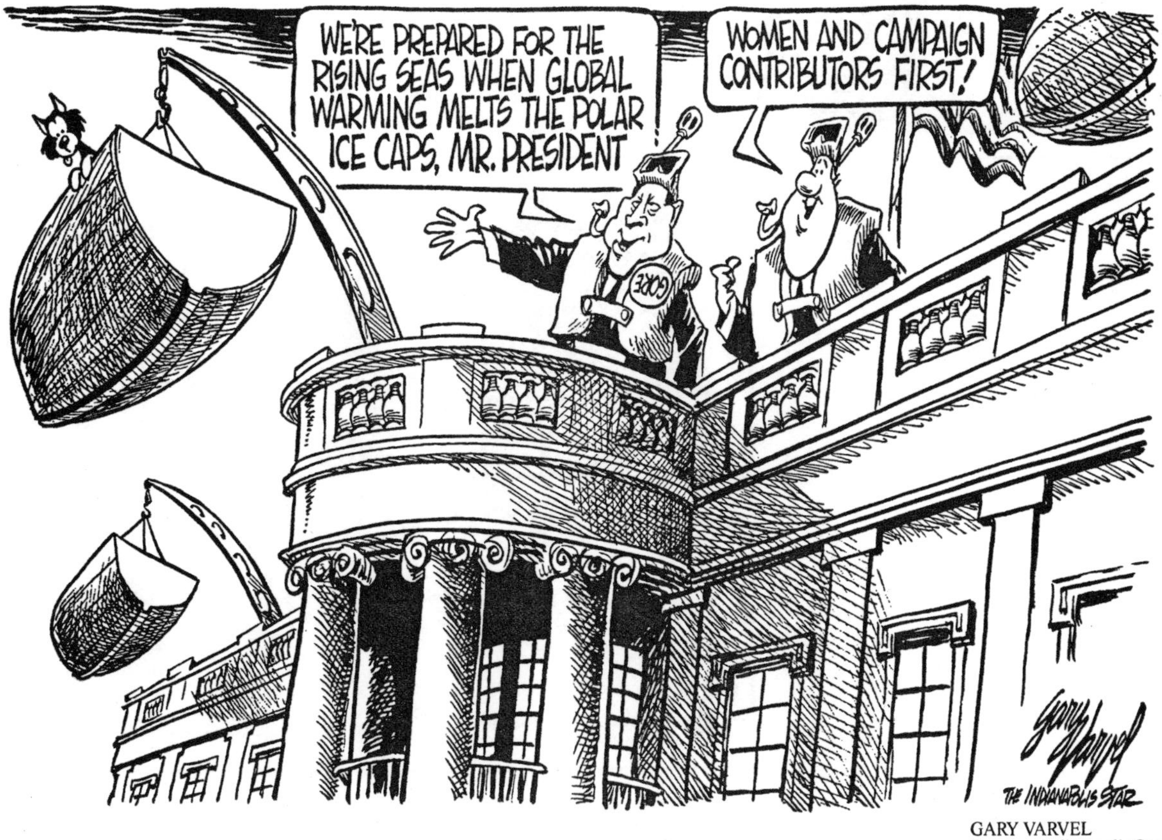
WE'RE PREPARED FOR THE RISING SEAS WHEN GLOBAL WARMING MELTS THE POLAR ICE CAPS, MR. PRESIDENT
WOMEN AND CAMPAIGN CONTRIBUTORS FIRST!
GORE
THE INDIANAPOLIS STAR

GARY VARVEL
Courtesy Indianapolis Star

STEVE SACK
Courtesy Minneapolis Star-Tribune

DICK WRIGHT
Courtesy Columbus Dispatch

ANN CLEAVES
Courtesy Palisadian Post

GLENN MCCOY
Courtesy Belleville News-Democrat

MICHAEL RAMIREZ
Courtesy Los Angeles Times

GARY MCCOY
Courtesy Suburban Journals (Ill.)

CLAY BENNETT
Courtesy North America Syndicate

STEVE GREENBERG
Courtesy Seattle Post-Intelligencer

GARY MCCOY
Courtesy Suburban Journals (Ill.)

..."EL NIÑO" FINDS ITS WAY into the AMERICAN VERNACULAR...

WALT HANDELSMAN
Courtesy New Orleans Times-Picayune

SCOTT BATEMAN
Courtesy North America Syndicate

JON RICHARDS
Courtesy Santa Fe Reporter

The Economy

The U.S. economy surged during 1997, and consumer and business confidence reached an all-time high. It was growth without inflation, and the federal budget deficit shrank substantially. Capital investment climbed to record levels, and employment continued to grow. Federal Reserve Chairman Alan Greenspan was moved to issue a stern warning about excesses to the bulls on Wall Street, but after a slight dip the market soared once again.

Asia's economy presented a different story, with stock markets plunging throughout the continent. Japan suffered its worst recession since World War II. Both North and South Korea seemed to be economic basket cases, and the economy of China lost much of its steam.

Restrictive new Environmental Protection Agency regulations to save endangered species forced many businesses to close, and several large companies were accused of using child labor overseas. President Clinton pushed for "fast-track" legislation to allow him to negotiate trade agreements more freely with other nations, and a crippling UPS strike showed that labor had regained some of its old clout.

The Justice Department sued Microsoft and founder Bill Gates over the company's business practices. Attorney General Janet Reno also threatened to assess the company with millions in fines.

ED GAMBLE
Courtesy Florida Times-Union

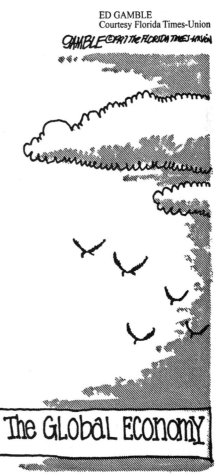

The GLOBAL ECONOMY

STEADY AS SHE GOES

BALANCED BUDGET

THE ECONOMY

DRAPER HILL
Courtesy Detroit News

THEN...

HAVE TO PAY FOR MY BABYBOOMER CHILDREN!

NOW...

HAVE TO PAY FOR MY BABY BOOMER PARENTS!

JAMES GRASDAL
Courtesy Edmonton Journal

JEFF STAHLER
Courtesy Cincinnati Post

STAHLER.
©THE CINCINNATI POST '97

I MISS THE FIVE & DIME ERA

DAVID GRANLUND
Courtesy Middlesex News (Mass.)

JEFF DANZIGER
Courtesy Los Angeles Times Syndicate

BOB DORNFRIED
Courtesy Fairfield Citizen

KIRK ANDERSON
Courtesy St. Paul Pioneer Press

TAKING THE BITE OUT OF AN APPLE...

ANNETTE BALESTERI
Courtesy Antioch Ledger-Dispatch (Calif.)

140

STEVE LINDSTROM
Courtesy Duluth News-Tribune

SCOTT WILLIS
Courtesy San Jose Mercury News

KIRK ANDERSON
Courtesy St. Paul Pioneer Press

Report Says Nike Workers in Vietnam Paid Starvation Wages and
Suffer Corporal Punishment and Forced Running Inflicted by Managers

JEFF DANZIGER
Courtesy Los Angeles Times Syndicate

ETTA HULME
Courtesy Fort Worth Star-Telegram

PAUL FELL
Courtesy Lincoln Journal Star

STEVE BREEN
Courtesy Asbury Park Press

JAMES GRASDAL
Courtesy Edmonton Journal

EDGAR SOLLER
Courtesy California Examiner

144

ROGER SCHILLERSTROM
Courtesy Crain Communications (Ill.)

JAMES CASCIARI
Courtesy Vero Beach Press Journal

JOE HOFFECKER
Courtesy Cincinnati Business Courier

"GO BACK TO SLEEP, ALAN... IF THERE IS A MONSTER IN YOUR CLOSET, IT'S ONLY A LITTLE ONE!"

JIM JORDAN
Courtesy Elmhurst Press (Ill.)

JOHN SHERFFIUS
Courtesy Ventura County Star

SCOTT STANTIS
Courtesy Birmingham News

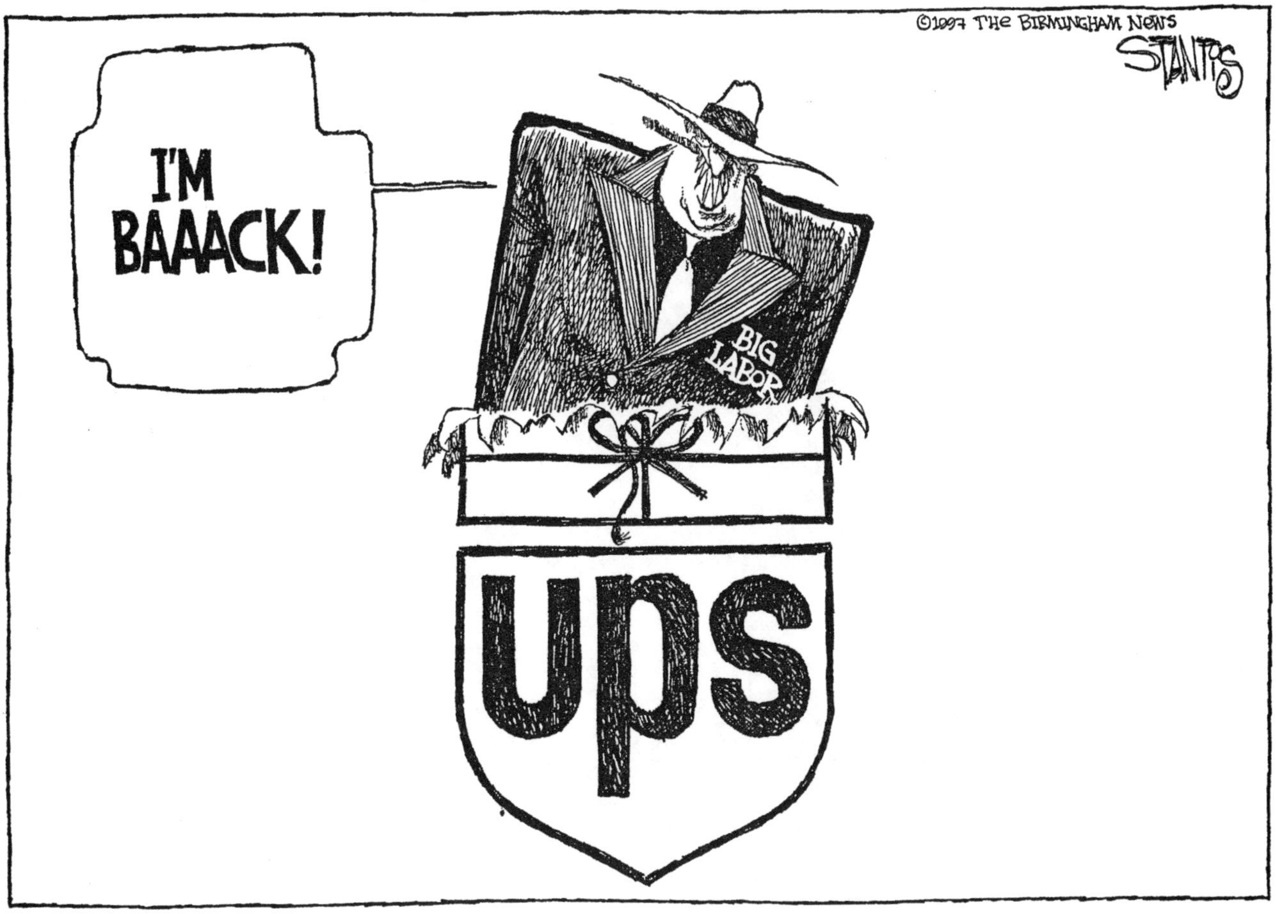
©1997 THE BIRMINGHAM NEWS
STANTIS
I'M BAAACK!
BIG LABOR
UPS

PAUL FELL
Courtesy Lincoln Journal Star

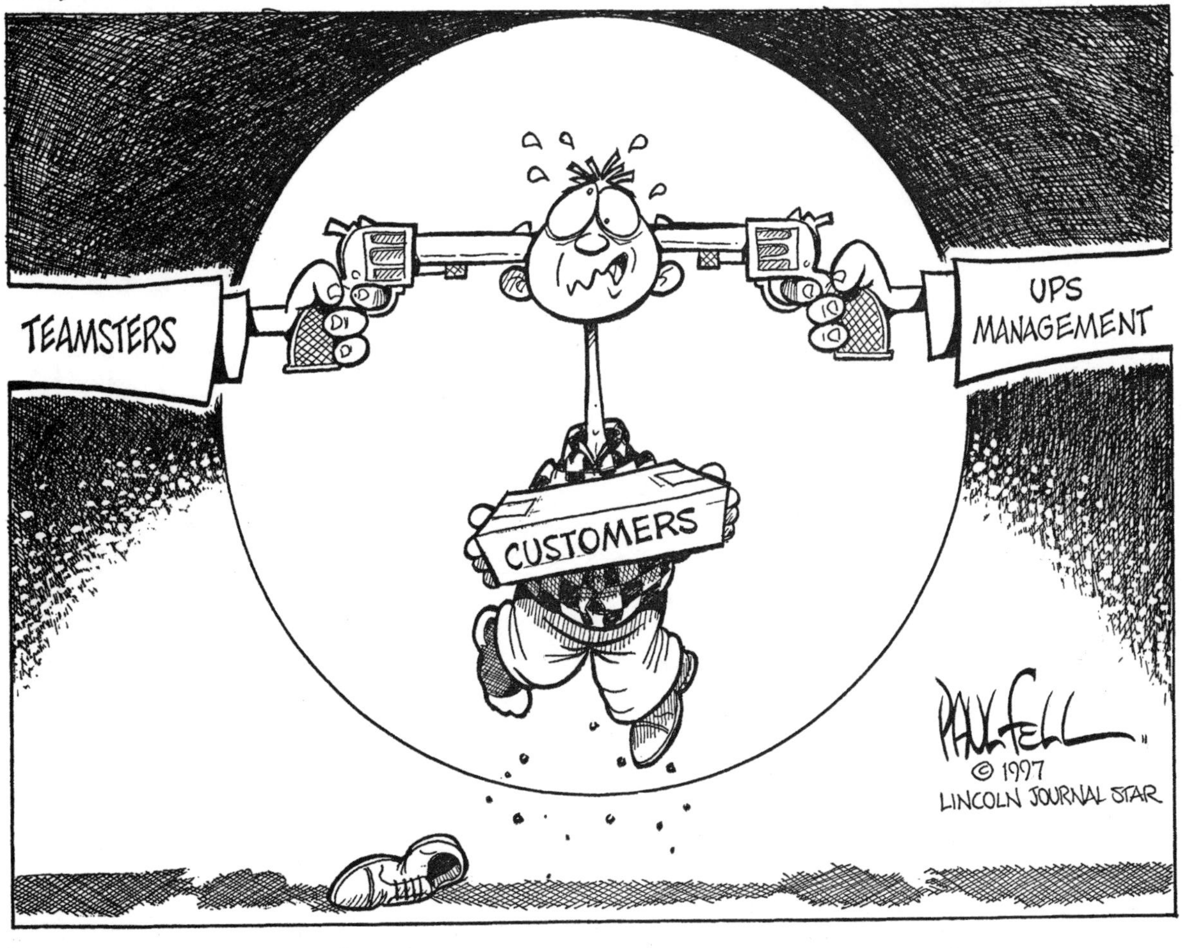
TEAMSTERS
UPS MANAGEMENT
CUSTOMERS
PAUL FELL
© 1997
LINCOLN JOURNAL STAR

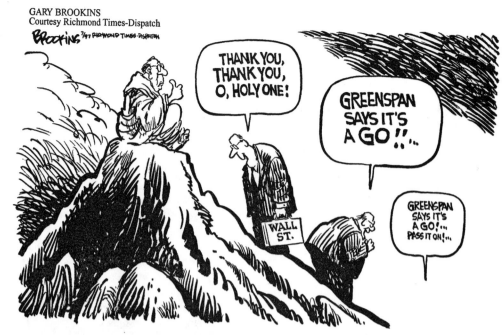

GARY BROOKINS
Courtesy Richmond Times-Dispatch

BOB GORRELL
Courtesy Richmond Times-Dispatch

"ALAN GREENSPAN SENT ME...!"

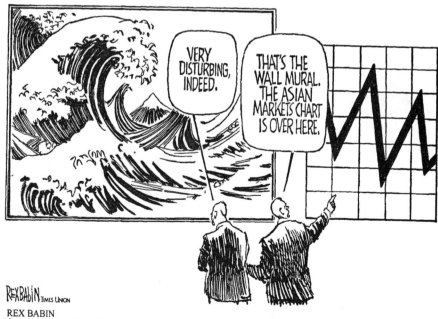

REX BABIN
Courtesy Albany Times Union

BILL WHITEHEAD
Courtesy Kansas City Business Journal

DENNIS DRAUGHON
Courtesy Scranton Times

BILL GARNER
Courtesy Washington Times

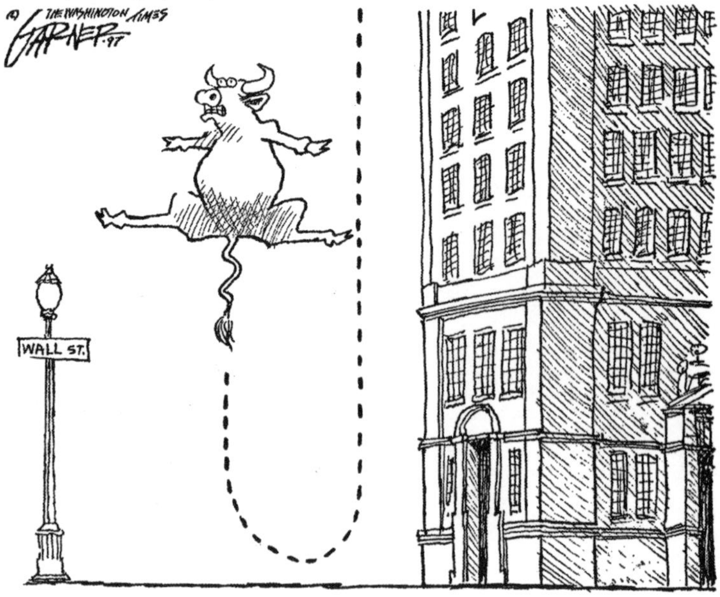
© THE WASHINGTON TIMES GARNER '97
WALL ST.

JIM BUSH
Courtesy Providence Journal-Bulletin

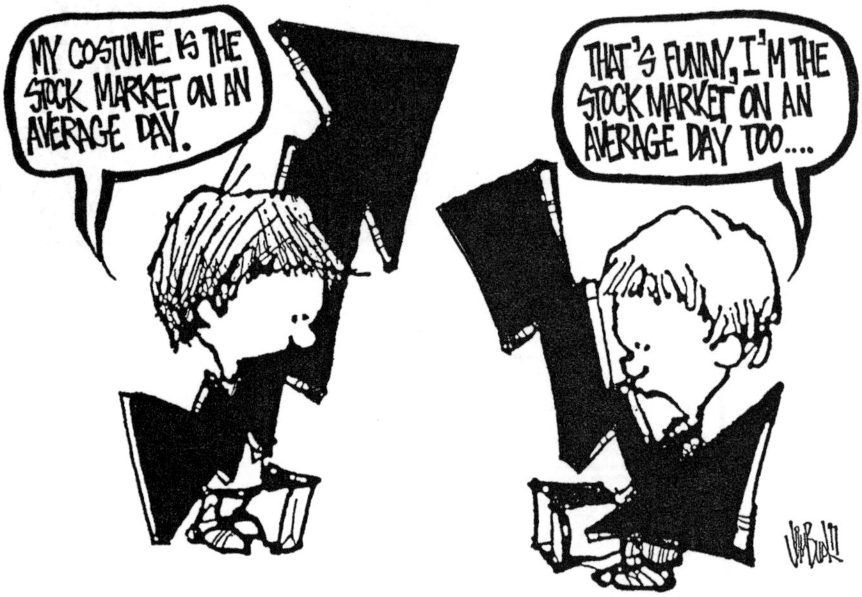
MY COSTUME IS THE STOCK MARKET ON AN AVERAGE DAY.
THAT'S FUNNY, I'M THE STOCK MARKET ON AN AVERAGE DAY TOO....

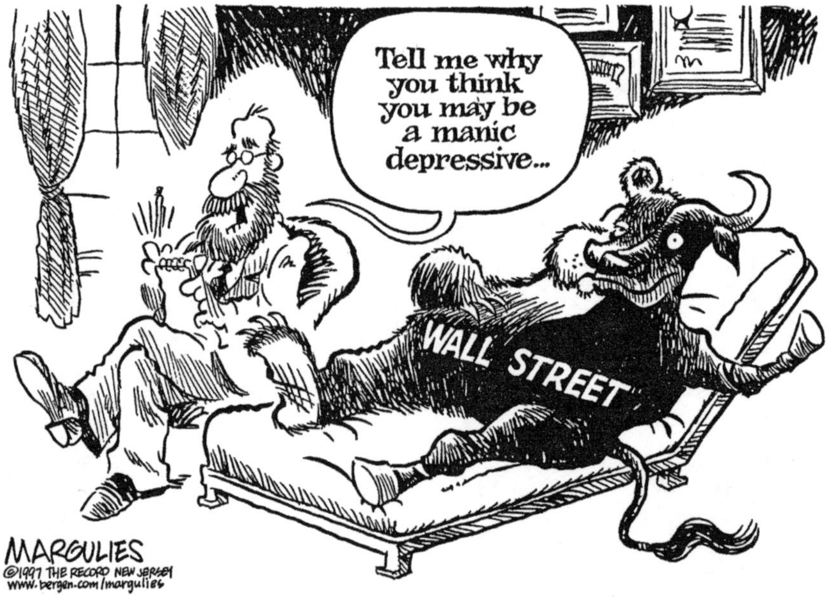
Tell me why you think you may be a manic depressive...
WALL STREET
MARGULIES
©1997 THE RECORD NEW JERSEY
www.bergen.com/margulies

JIMMY MARGULIES
Courtesy The Record (N.J.)

ED STEIN
Courtesy Rocky Mountain News

GENE PAYNE
Courtesy Charlotte Observer

MARLBORO COUNTRY

JOHN J. KNUDSEN
Courtesy St. Louis Review

Health

After many years of litigation over the effects of smoking, tobacco companies agreed to a settlement with a group of state attorneys general. The landmark, $360-billion agreement marked the end of Joe Camel, the Marlboro Man, cigarette vending machines, tobacco billboard advertisements, and sports events sponsored by Big Tobacco.

More and more in 1997 Americans were switching their family health insurance coverage to health maintenance organizations, largely because of lower costs. Many feared, however, that the quality of their health care would decline as decision-making shifts from doctors to managed-care administrators. Policy holders found other drawbacks as well: a limited choice of doctors and hospitals and waiting periods to receive care.

For the first time the nation's largest physicians group, the American Medical Association, agreed to endorse a consumer health-care producer, in this case the Sunbeam Corporation. The AMA later asked to be released from the agreement, but Sunbeam declined. Sunbeam announced that it expected the AMA to honor the contract and would take "all necessary actions" to protect its interests.

In a few years, so-called Baby Boomers will begin to retire, and some experts fear that the large numbers of retirees may push the annual costs of Medicare and Social Security through the roof.

Dr. Jack Kevorkian, also known as Dr. Death, continued his efforts to help the terminally ill realize a quicker demise.

MIKE SMITH
Courtesy United Feature Syndicate

BOB RICH
Courtesy Connecticut Post

VIC CANTONE
Courtesy King Features /
North America Syndicate

BUTT END OF CRUEL JOKE

JOHN SPENCER
Courtesy Philadelphia Business Journal

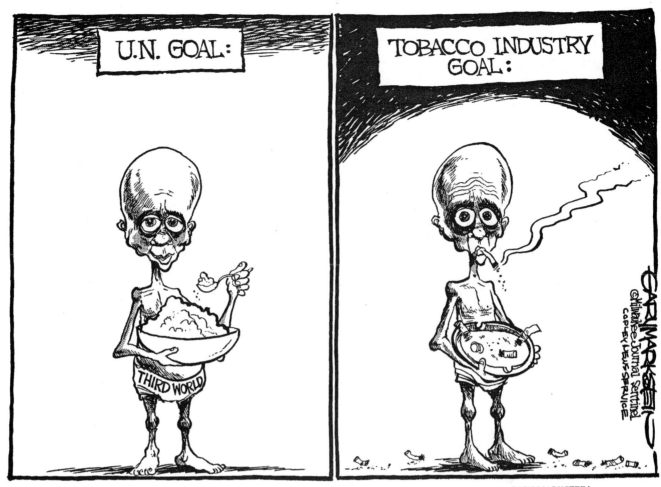

GARY MARKSTEIN
Courtesy Milwaukee Journal Sentinel

STEVE KELLEY
Courtesy San Diego Union-Tribune

OBITUARIES

Joe Camel, 45; Cigarett

Joseph S. "Smokin' Joe" Camel died yesterday. He was 45 (9 human years). Only recently doctors discovered the two lumps on his back were malignant and inoperable.

In effect, walking a mile, for this camel, was no longer possible.

He leaves no known survivors.

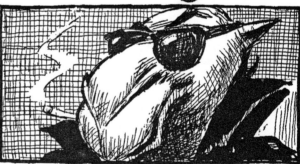

Cigarette "Smokesman"

In lieu of flowers, contributions to the American Cancer Society (No cigarette coupons please). His ashes will be scattered at a nearby playlot.

IT'S NOT MY FAULT....
IT'S ADDICTIVE !

GENE PAYNE
Courtesy Charlotte Observer

KEVIN KALLAUGHER
Courtesy Baltimore Sun

DAVID DONAR
Courtesy Macomb Daily

JIM BERRY
Courtesy NEA

V. CULLUM ROGERS
Courtesy Durham Independent

MARK PETT
Courtesy Deseret News (Utah)

ROB ROGERS
Courtesy Pittsburgh Post-Gazette

ED FISCHER
Courtesy Rochester Post-Bulletin

DAVID GRANLUND
Courtesy Middlesex News (Mass.)

JOHN MARSHALL
Courtesy Binghampton Press and Sun-Bulletin

LARRY WRIGHT
Courtesy Detroit News

JERRY BARNETT
Courtesy Indianapolis News

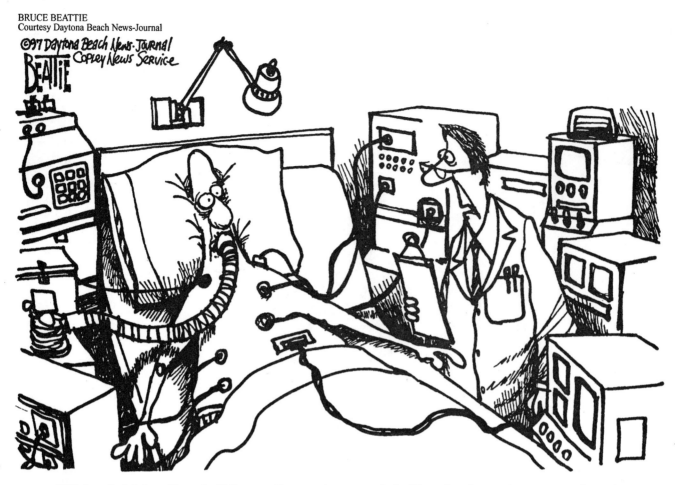

"This right-to-die stuff is pretty controversial. Too bad you're not a dog."

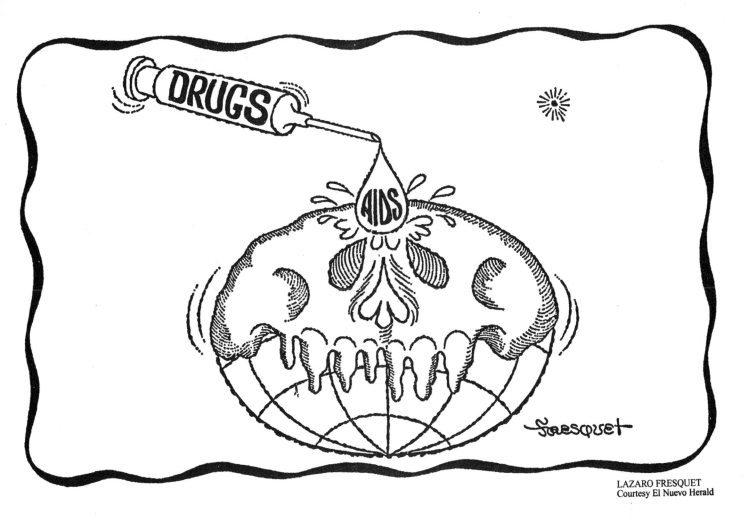

LAZARO FRESQUET
Courtesy El Nuevo Herald

MICHAEL RAMIREZ
Courtesy Los Angeles Times

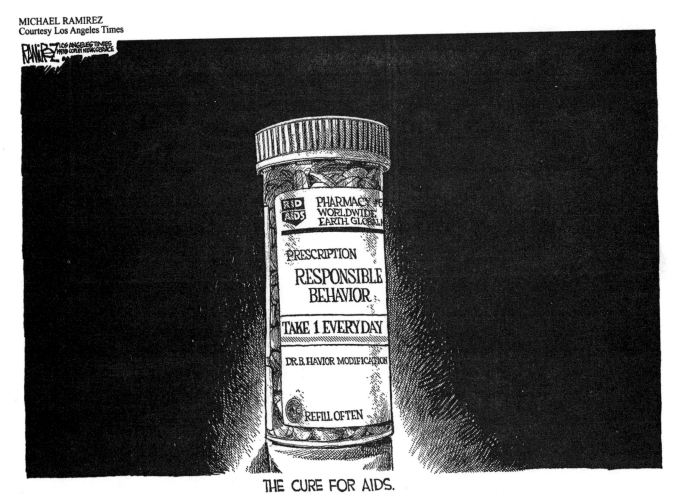

THE CURE FOR AIDS.

163

ROGER SCHILLERSTROM
Courtesy Crain Communications (Ill.)

EDWARD COLLEY
Courtesy Memorial Press Group

GILL FOX
Courtesy Norwalk Citizen-News

STEVE MCBRIDE
Courtesy Independence Daily Reporter (Kan.)

STEVE LINDSTROM
Courtesy Duluth News-Tribune

VIC CANTONE
Courtesy King Features /
North America Syndicate

VIC CANTONE
B.P. PUBLICATIONS
EMERGENCY ROOM
PLEASE TAKE A NUMBER
HMO
MEDICARE
23
HOSPITALS IN $$ PAIN
HOLDING PATTERN

GENE PAYNE
Courtesy Charlotte Observer

THE PRESIDENT DENIES EVER KNOWING YOU AND IF DID, HE DENIES ANY KNOWLEDGE OF PROMISES TO BE ANYTHING MORE THAN JUST ACQUAINTANCES
HEALTH CARE
ASSISTANT TO THE PRESIDENT
PAYNE

The GROWTH INDUSTRY OF THE NEXT MILLENNIUM:
HMO DEPOT
DO-IT-YOURSELF HEALTH CARE!
SALE SURGICAL SUPPLIES
I.V.'s 29.99 DOZ
HOW-TO BOOKS LARGEST SELECTION!
I PICKED UP EVERYTHING I NEED TO DO MY OWN APPENDECTOMY!
...I'M PUTTIN' IN A NEW HIP THIS WEEKEND!
WILLIS ©1997 SAN JOSE MERCURY NEWS

SCOTT WILLIS
Courtesy San Jose Mercury News

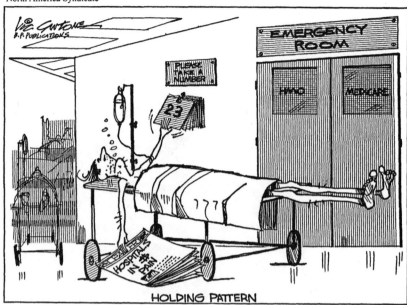

JOE MAJESKI
Courtesy Sunday Dispatch (Pa.)

MIKE LUCKOVICH
Courtesy Atlanta Constitution

WES RAND
Courtesy Norwich Bulletin

ED FISCHER
Courtesy Rochester Post-Bulletin

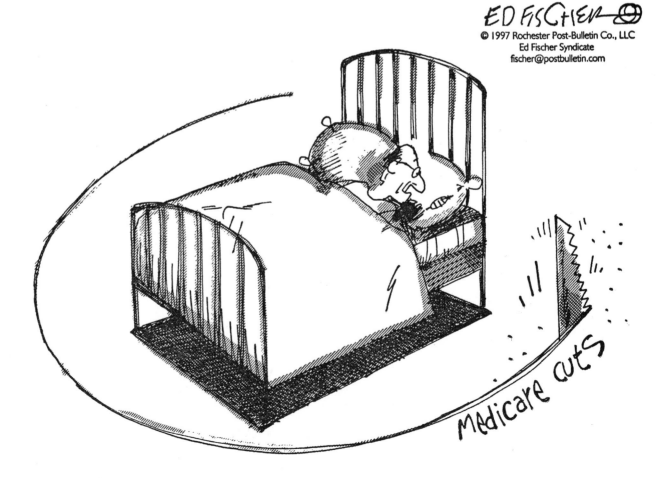

Space and Air Travel

The Russian space station Mir suffered a number of problems during the year, including a collision with a remote-controlled cargo ship and a main computer that repeatedly shut down. The space shuttle Atlantis was sent to rendezvous with Mir, bringing a fresh American astronaut with urgently needed repair equipment.

Several U.S. congressmen opposed sending more Americans to the troubled satellite, contending that Russia was using the aging Mir to obtain transfusions of money to keep its sagging space industry alive.

UFO enthusiasts convened at Roswell, New Mexico, to commemorate what many claim was a visit by aliens fifty years ago. Air Force officials held a press conference to put the matter to rest "once and for all," but merely raised new questions about the incident.

NASA's Sojourner landed on Mars and sent back spectacular photographs of the red planet.

Aircraft companies confronted the problem of constantly increasing air traffic and the need to design and build larger airplanes. But the question remained: How large can you build an airplane that will still be safe?

JAMES MCCLOSKEY
Courtesy Staunton Daily News Leader

169

JIM BORGMAN
Courtesy Cincinnati Enquirer

" YOU MEAN WE'VE BEEN KEEPING CRASH TEST DUMMIES ON LIFE SUPPORT IN A HANGAR AT WRIGHT-PATTERSON FOR FIFTY YEARS ?! "

GEORGE DANBY
Courtesy Bangor Daily News

ART HENRIKSON
Courtesy Des Plaines Daily Herald

WALT HANDELSMAN
Courtesy New Orleans Times-Picayune

171

JACK JURDEN
Courtesy Wilmington News Journal

MIKE KEEFE
Courtesy Denver Post

JERRY HOLBERT
Courtesy Boston Herald

GARY VARVEL
Courtesy Indianapolis Star

JERRY HOLBERT
Courtesy Boston Herald

MARSHALL RAMSEY
Courtesy Jackson Clarion-Ledger

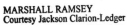

THE SHADOW AND THE IMAGE

Sports

Tiger Woods, a 21-year-old golfer of black and Asian-American parentage, took the sports world by storm when he easily won the fabled Masters Golf Tournament. His triumph came just two days before the fiftieth anniversary of Jackie Robinson's historic debut in major league baseball.

The world of boxing also glimpsed something shocking. A bout for the world heavyweight championship was stopped in the third round after challenger Mike Tyson bit chunks out of the ears of champion Evander Holyfield. Referee Mills Lane reluctantly disqualified Tyson, a former champion. The Nevada State Boxing Commission later fined Tyson $3 million and revoked his license to box for a year.

National Basketball Association star Latrell Sprewell of the Golden State Warriors was suspended for one year after choking and threatening his coach, P.J. Carlesimo.

Various other well-known sports figures found themselves involved in various degrees of drug use, wife-beating, criminal acts, and general bending of the rules. At least some fans and media are calling for strict enforcement of rules and stiffer penalties for outrageous behavior on and off the playing field.

JACK HIGGINS
Courtesy Chicago Sun-Times

I now realize my fight with HOLYFIELD was a situation where I bit off more than I could chew.

STEVE MCBRIDE
Courtesy Independence Daily Reporter (Kan.)

OK WHO THE @#!! FORGOT TO FEED HIM BEFORE THE FIGHT?

FRED CURATOLO
Courtesy Edmonton Sun

TYSON CONTINUES TO TRAIN, DESPITE HIS SUSPENSION...

MIKE LUCKOVICH
Courtesy Atlanta Constitution

CHIP BOK
Courtesy Akron Beacon Journal

SCOTT WILLIS
Courtesy San Jose Mercury News

JOE HOFFECKER
Courtesy Cincinnati Business Courier

"I REALIZE IT SEEMS RADICAL... BUT DEEP DOWN, IT'S STILL YOUR LEXUS."

WILL O'TOOLE
Courtesy Home News & Tribune (N.J.)

STEVE YORK
Courtesy Kankakee Daily Journal

SVEN VAN ASSCHE
Courtesy Darien Times

BARBARA BRANDON
Courtesy Universal Press Syndicate

EDWARD COLLEY
Courtesy Memorial Press Group

JOE LONG
Courtesy Little Falls Evening Times (N.Y.)

Canada

The Helms-Burton Act, which punishes companies that invest in Cuba, was held largely responsible for the high jobless rate in Canada during the year. Cuba is one of Canada's largest trading partners, and the restraints Helms-Burton put on industry has been a sore point with politicians, businesses, and the media.

Prime Minister Jean Cretien won a slim victory in early June, but the net result of the election was a weakened central government and a stronger position for independence-minded Quebec. France, however, remained aloof in Quebec's push for separation.

The salmon fishing treaty with the United States continued to frustrate Canadian fishermen. The group claims that the U.S. is overfishing and reducing the number of salmon bound for Canadian rivers and streams to spawn.

Canada's only toxic waste disposal site was plagued by leaks during 1997. The Red Cross attempted to block the Krever Report, which assigned blame and named names in a scandal involving tainted blood. Organized crime, said to be growing throughout the world, sought ways to infiltrate Canada during the year, and a postal strike helped slow the nation's economy.

Len Norris, 83, long-time editorial cartoonist for the Vancouver Sun, died on August 12. He was a master of biting social satire.

ROY PETERSON
Courtesy Vancouver Sun

STEVE NEASE
Courtesy St. John's Telegram

IF CANADA WERE SEPTUPLETS

YUKON · NWT · BC · PRAIRIES · ONT · QUE · MARITIMES

FRED CURATOLO
Courtesy Edmonton Sun

EVERY FEW YEARS THE IRAQIS AND AMERICANS PLAY THEIR GAME OF BRINKMANSHIP.

—AND WE PLAY OURS.

DEATH TO U.S.A.

CUPW ON STRIKE

STEVE NEASE
Courtesy Montreal Gazette

5 solitudes

CANADA

THE whole IS greater THAN THE sum OF ITS parties...

JOSH BEUTEL
Courtesy New Brunswick
Evening Times-Globe

DENNY PRITCHARD
Courtesy Montreal Gazette

ROY PETERSON
Courtesy Vancouver Sun

DAN MURPHY
Courtesy Vancouver Province

JOSH BEUTEL
Courtesy Le Journal

MALCOLM MAYES
Courtesy Edmonton Journal

BILL HOGAN
Courtesy New Brunswick
Times-Transcript

JAMES GRASDAL
Courtesy Edmonton Journal

185

I WANT YOURS!

BC SALMON

STEVE NEASE
Courtesy St. John's Telegram

DAN MURPHY
Courtesy Vancouver Province

DENNY PRITCHARD
Courtesy Ottawa Citizen

only one doctorate?!

DISHWASHER WANTED

SPIKES DINER

RESUME

Pritchard © 97.

DAN MURPHY
Courtesy Vancouver Province

BILL HOGAN
Courtesy New Brunswick Times-Transcript

SCOTT STANTIS
Courtesy Birmingham News

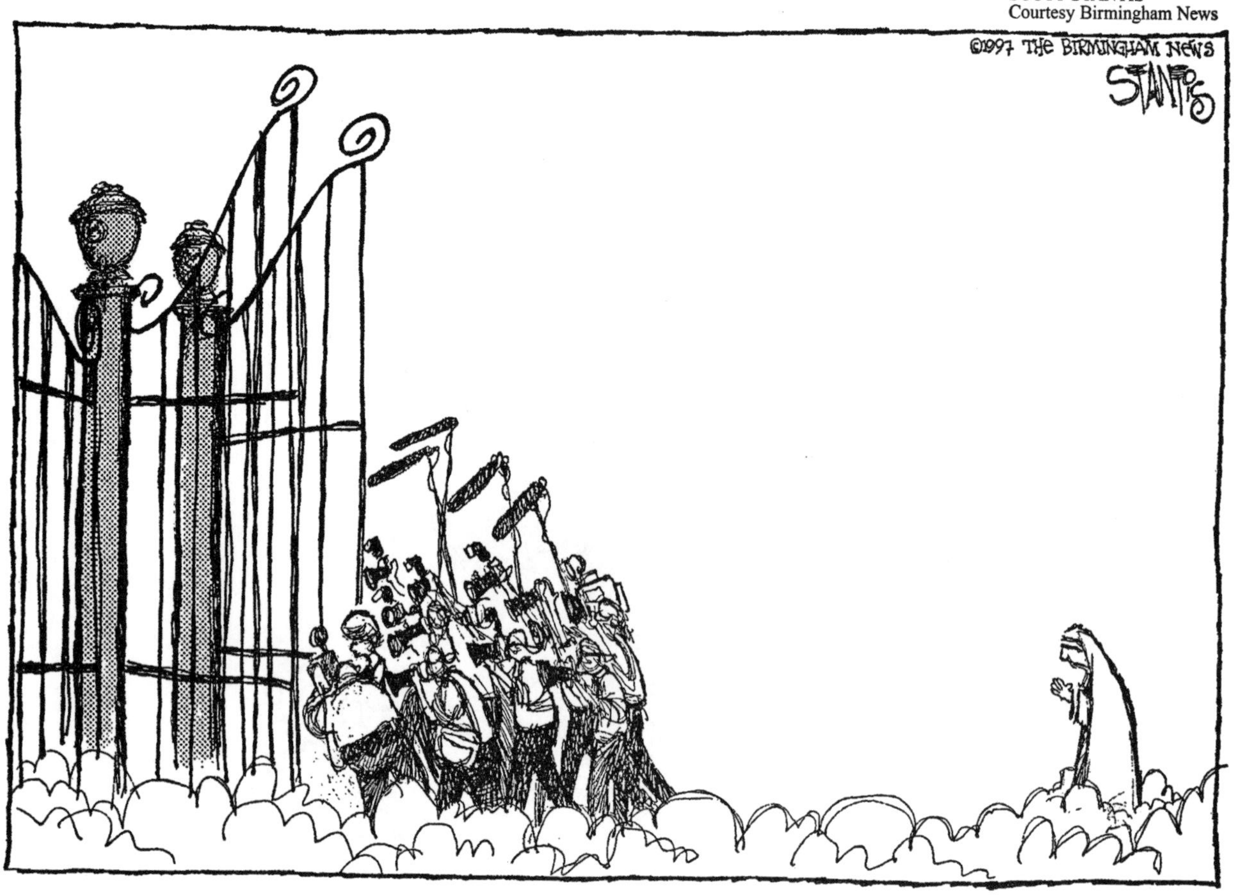

©1997 THE BIRMINGHAM NEWS
STANTIS

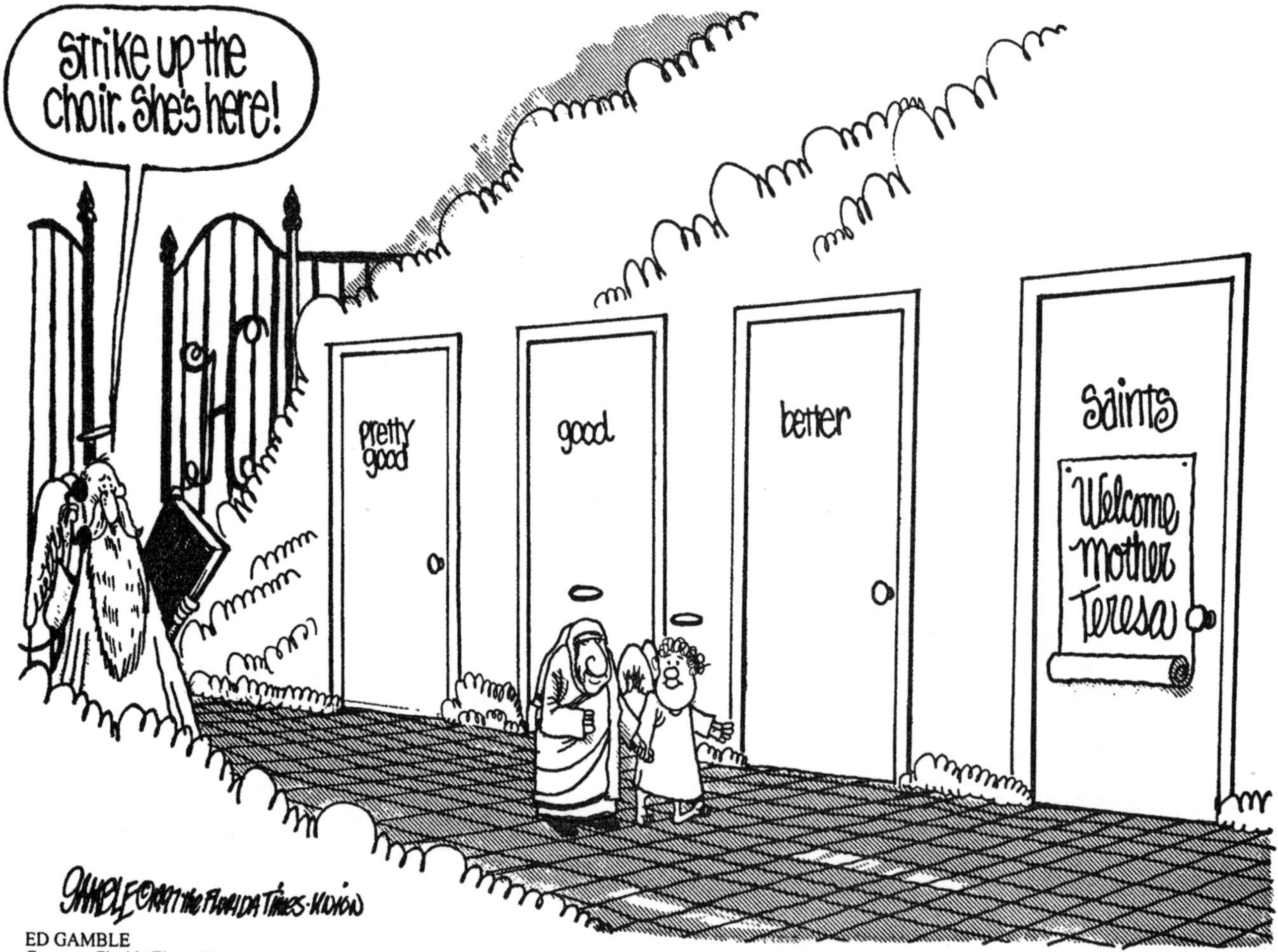

Strike up the choir. She's here!
pretty good
good
better
Saints
Welcome Mother Teresa
GAMBLE ©1997 the Florida Times-Union

ED GAMBLE
Courtesy Florida Times-Union

... and Other Issues

Britain's Princess Diana, her millionaire escort Dodi Fayed, and their chauffeur were killed in an automobile crash in a Paris tunnel. A horde of paparazzi who were chasing her limousine at speeds of more than 100 miles an hour, were blamed for the crash, along with her driver, who police said was drunk. Shortly before Diana's funeral, Mother Teresa, the revered Catholic nun who had devoted her life to helping the poorest of the poor in India, also died following an extended illness.

Scottish researchers cloned an adult mammal, a sheep named Dolly, from a single cell. The O. J. Simpson case finally closed when a jury found him guilty of the deaths of his wife, Nicole, and her friend, Ron Goldman. Simpson was ordered to pay $33.5 million to the families of the murder victims.

Television mogul Ted Turner gave a billion dollars to the United Nations with "no strings attached," and sportscaster Marv Albert pleaded guilty to assault and battery charges after a woman accused him of sexual assault. The Hooters restaurant chain was allowed to continue hiring only female waitresses after settling with two men who had charged sexual discrimination.

Notables who died in 1997 included actors Robert Mitchum and Jimmy Stewart, comedian Red Skelton, novelist James Michener, singer-actor John Denver, and ocean explorer Jacques Cousteau.

MALCOLM MAYES
Courtesy Edmonton Journal

RICHARD WALLMEYER
Courtesy Long Beach Press-Telegram

JON RICHARDS
Courtesy Santa Fe Reporter

BACKSTAGE AT THE AUCTION OF MOTHER TERESA'S CLOTHES

DANIEL AGUILA
Courtesy Filipino Reporter

el Dani's DENIZENS – "HEAVENLY BUDDIES"

©1997 NY FILIPINO REPORTER

...TWO OF A KIND, WITH ONE MIND...

MOTHER TERESA (1910-1997)   PRINCESS DIANA (1961-1997)

JOHN SHERFFIUS
Courtesy Ventura County Star

MIKE KEEFE
Courtesy Denver Post

THE BRITISH CROWN HAS LOST A PRIZE JEWEL

CANDLE IN THE 'WIND'

TOM BECK
Courtesy Freeport Journal-Standard

LOU GRANT
Courtesy The Montclarion (Calif.)

J.R. ROSE
Courtesy Byrd Newspapers (Va.)

MARK STREETER
Courtesy Savannah Morning News

STEVE BREEN
Courtesy Asbury Park Press

MICHAEL RAMIREZ
Courtesy Memphis Commercial Appeal

ANN TELNAES
Courtesy Newsday

JEFF KOTERBA
Courtesy Omaha World-Herald

"HEAR THE BELLS RINGING, HARVEY?... HE'S GOING TO GET HIS WINGS..."

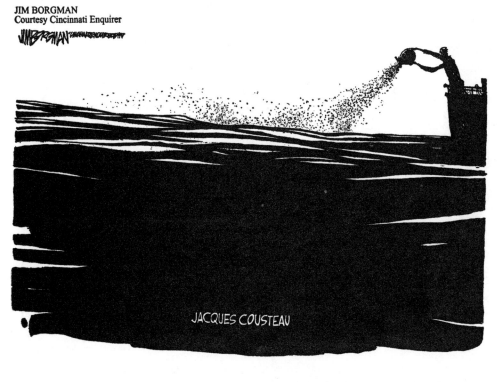

JACQUES COUSTEAU

STEVE MCBRIDE
Courtesy Independence Daily Reporter (Kan.)

NEIL GRAHAME
Courtesy Spencer Newspapers

198

BOB GORRELL
Courtesy Richmond Times-Dispatch

STEVE KELLEY
Courtesy San Diego Union-Tribune

GUY BADEAUX
Courtesy Le Droit, Ottawa

JOE LONG
Courtesy Little Falls
Evening Times (N.Y.)

CHAN LOWE
Courtesy Fort Lauderdale Sun-Sentinel

S.C. RAWLS
Courtesy Rockdale Citizen

MIKE PETERS
Courtesy Dayton Daily News

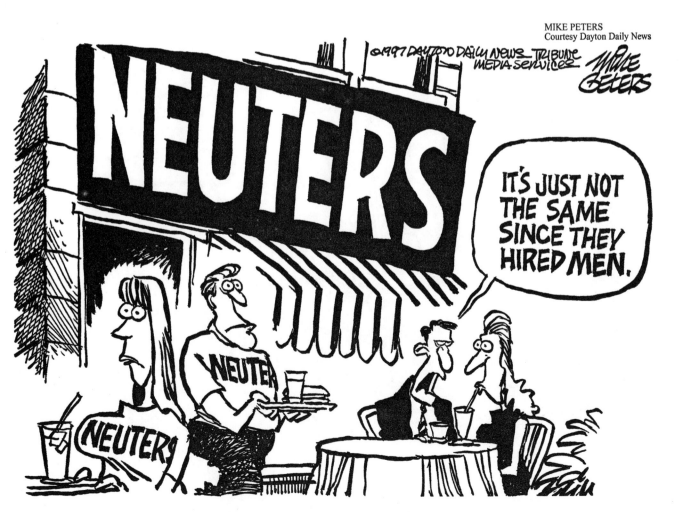

RANDY BISH
Courtesy Greensburg Tribune-Review (Pa.)

TOM GIBB
Courtesy Altoona Tribune-Democrat

Past Award Winners

NATIONAL HEADLINER AWARD

1938—C.D. Batchelor, New York Daily News
1939—John Knott, Dallas News
1940—Herbert Block, NEA
1941—Charles H. Sykes, Philadelphia Evening Ledger
1942—Jerry Doyle, Philadelphia Record
1943—Vaughn Shoemaker, Chicago Daily News
1944—Roy Justus, Sioux City Journal
1945—F.O. Alexander, Philadelphia Bulletin
1946—Hank Barrow, Associated Press
1947—Cy Hungerford, Pittsburgh Post-Gazette
1948—Tom Little, Nashville Tennessean
1949—Bruce Russell, Los Angeles Times
1950—Dorman Smith, NEA
1951—C.G. Werner, Indianapolis Star
1952—John Fischetti, NEA
1953—James T. Berryman and
        Gib Crocket, Washington Star
1954—Scott Long, Minneapolis Tribune
1955—Leo Thiele, Los Angeles Mirror-News
1956—John Milt Morris, Associated Press
1957—Frank Miller, Des Moines Register
1958—Burris Jenkins, Jr., New York Journal-American
1959—Karl Hubenthal, Los Angeles Examiner
1960—Don Hesse, St. Louis Globe-Democrat
1961—L.D. Warren, Cincinnati Enquirer
1962—Franklin Morse, Los Angeles Mirror
1963—Charles Bissell, Nashville Tennessean
1964—Lou Grant, Oakland Tribune
1965—Merle R. Tingley, London (Ont.) Free Press
1966—Hugh Haynie, Louisville Courier-Journal
1967—Jim Berry, NEA
1968—Warren King, New York News
1969—Larry Barton, Toledo Blade
1970—Bill Crawford, NEA
1971—Ray Osrin, Cleveland Plain Dealer
1972—Jacob Burck, Chicago Sun-Times
1973—Ranan Lurie, New York Times
1974—Tom Darcy, Newsday
1975—Bill Sanders, Milwaukee Journal
1976—No award given
1977—Paul Szep, Boston Globe
1978—Dwane Powell, Raleigh News and Observer
1979—Pat Oliphant, Washington Star
1980—Don Wright, Miami News
1981—Bill Garner, Memphis Commercial Appeal
1982—Mike Peters, Dayton Daily News
1983—Doug Marlette, Charlotte Observer
1984—Steve Benson, Arizona Republic
1985—Bill Day, Detroit Free Press
1986—Mike Keefe, Denver Post
1987—Mike Peters, Dayton Daily News
1988—Doug Marlette, Charlotte Observer
1989—Walt Handelsman, Scranton Times
1990—Robert Ariail, The State
1991—Jim Borgman, Cincinnati Enquirer

1992—Mike Luckovich, Atlanta Constitution
1993—Walt Handelsman, New Orleans Times-Picayune
1994—Mike Peters, Dayton Daily News
1995—Rob Rogers, Pittsburgh Post-Gazette
1996—Jimmy Margulies, The Record, New Jersey
1997—Ann Telnaes, North America Syndicate

PULITZER PRIZE

1922—Rollin Kirby, New York World
1923—No award given
1924—J.N. Darling, New York Herald-Tribune
1925—Rollin Kirby, New York World
1926—D.R. Fitzpatrick, St. Louis Post-Dispatch
1927—Nelson Harding, Brooklyn Eagle
1928—Nelson Harding, Brooklyn Eagle
1929—Rollin Kirby, New York World
1930—Charles Macauley, Brooklyn Eagle
1931—Edmund Duffy, Baltimore Sun
1932—John T. McCutcheon, Chicago Tribune
1933—H.M. Talburt, Washington Daily News
1934—Edmund Duffy, Baltimore Sun
1935—Ross A. Lewis, Milwaukee Journal
1936—No award given
1937—C.D. Batchelor, New York Daily News
1938—Vaughn Shoemaker, Chicago Daily News
1939—Charles G. Werner, Daily Oklahoman
1940—Edmund Duffy, Baltimore Sun
1941—Jacob Burck, Chicago Times
1942—Herbert L. Block, NEA
1943—Jay N. Darling, New York Herald-Tribune
1944—Clifford K. Berryman, Washington Star
1945—Bill Mauldin, United Features Syndicate
1946—Bruce Russell, Los Angeles Times
1947—Vaughn Shoemaker, Chicago Daily News
1948—Reuben L. ("Rube") Goldberg, New York Sun
1949—Lute Pease, Newark Evening News
1950—James T. Berryman, Washington Star
1951—Reginald W. Manning, Arizona Republic
1952—Fred L. Packer, New York Mirror
1953—Edward D. Kuekes, Cleveland Plain Dealer
1954—Herbert L. Block, Washington Post
1955—Daniel R. Fitzpatrick, St. Louis Post-Dispatch
1956—Robert York, Louisville Times
1957—Tom Little, Nashville Tennessean
1958—Bruce M. Shanks, Buffalo Evening News
1959—Bill Mauldin, St. Louis Post-Dispatch
1960—No award given
1961—Carey Orr, Chicago Tribune
1962—Edmund S. Valtman, Hartford Times
1963—Frank Miller, Des Moines Register
1964—Paul Conrad, Denver Post
1965—No award given
1966—Don Wright, Miami News
1967—Patrick B. Oliphant, Denver Post
1968—Eugene Gray Payne, Charlotte Observer
1969—John Fischetti, Chicago Daily News
1970—Thomas F. Darcy, Newsday

1971—Paul Conrad, Los Angeles Times
1972—Jeffrey K. MacNelly, Richmond News Leader
1973—No award given
1974—Paul Szep, Boston Globe
1975—Garry Trudeau, Universal Press Syndicate
1976—Tony Auth, Philadelphia Enquirer
1977—Paul Szep, Boston Globe
1978—Jeff MacNelly, Richmond News Leader
1979—Herbert Block, Washington Post
1980—Don Wright, Miami News
1981—Mike Peters, Dayton Daily News
1982—Ben Sargent, Austin American-Statesman
1983—Dick Locher, Chicago Tribune
1984—Paul Conrad, Los Angeles Times
1985—Jeff MacNelly, Chicago Tribune
1986—Jules Feiffer, Universal Press Syndicate
1987—Berke Breathed, Washington Post Writers Group
1988—Doug Marlette, Atlanta Constitution
1989—Jack Higgins, Chicago Sun-Times
1990—Tom Toles, Buffalo News
1991—Jim Borgman, Cincinnati Enquirer
1992—Signe Wilkinson, Philadelphia Daily News
1993—Steve Benson, Arizona Republic
1994—Michael Ramirez, Memphis Commercial Appeal
1995—Mike Luckovich, Atlanta Constitution
1996—Jim Morin, Miami Herald
1997—Walt Handelsman, New Orleans Times-Picayune

NATIONAL NEWSPAPER AWARD/CANADA

1949—Jack Boothe, Toronto Globe and Mail
1950—James G. Reidford, Montreal Star
1951—Len Norris, Vancouver Sun
1952—Robert La Palme, Le Devoir, Montreal
1953—Robert W. Chambers, Halifax Chronicle-Herald
1954—John Collins, Montreal Gazette
1955—Merle R. Tingley, London Free Press
1956—James G. Reidford, Toronto Globe and Mail
1957—James G. Reidford, Toronto Globe and Mail
1958—Raoul Hunter, Le Soleil, Quebec
1959—Duncan Macpherson, Toronto Star
1960—Duncan Macpherson, Toronto Star
1961—Ed McNally, Montreal Star
1962—Duncan Macpherson, Toronto Star
1963—Jan Kamienski, Winnipeg Tribune
1964—Ed McNally, Montreal Star
1965—Duncan Macpherson, Toronto Star
1966—Robert W. Chambers, Halifax Chronicle-Herald

1967—Raoul Hunter, Le Soleil, Quebec
1968—Roy Peterson, Vancouver Sun
1969—Edward Uluschak, Edmonton Journal
1970—Duncan Macpherson, Toronto Daily Star
1971—Yardley Jones, Toronto Daily Star
1972—Duncan Macpherson, Toronto Star
1973—John Collins, Montreal Gazette
1974—Blaine, Hamilton Spectator
1975—Roy Peterson, Vancouver Sun
1976—Andy Donato, Toronto Sun
1977—Terry Mosher, Montreal Gazette
1978—Terry Mosher, Montreal Gazette
1979—Edd Uluschak, Edmonton Journal
1980—Vic Roschkov, Toronto Star
1981—Tom Innes, Calgary Herald
1982—Blaine, Hamilton Spectator
1983—Dale Cummings, Winnipeg Free Press
1984—Roy Peterson, Vancouver Sun
1985—Ed Franklin, Toronto Globe and Mail
1986—Brian Gable, Regina Leader-Post
1987—Raffi Anderian, Ottawa Citizen
1988—Vance Rodewalt, Calgary Herald
1989—Cameron Cardow, Regina Leader-Post
1990—Roy Peterson, Vancouver Sun
1991—Guy Badeaux, Le Droit, Ottawa
1992—Bruce Mackinnon, Halifax Herald
1993—Bruce Mackinnon, Halifax Herald
1994—Roy Peterson, Vancouver Sun
1995—Brian Gable, Toronto Globe and Mail
1996—Roy Peterson, Vancouver Sun

FISCHETTI AWARD

1982—Lee Judge, Kansas City Times
1983—Bill DeOre, Dallas Morning News
1984—Tom Toles, Buffalo News
1985—Scott Willis, Dallas Times-Herald
1986—Doug Marlette, Charlotte Observer
1987—Dick Locher, Chicago Tribune
1988—Arthur Bok, Akron Beacon-Journal
1989—Lambert Der, Greenville News
1990—Jeff Stahler, Cincinnati Post
1991—Mike Keefe, Denver Post
1992—Doug Marlette, New York Newsday
1993—Bill Schorr, Kansas City Star
1994—John Deering, Arkansas Democrat-Gazette
1995—Stuart Carlson, Milwaukee Journal Sentinel
1996—Jimmy Margulies, The Record, New Jersey
1997—Gary Markstein, Milwaukee Journal Sentinel

Index of Cartoonists

INDEX OF CARTOONISTS